MANGA UNIVERSITY

presents...

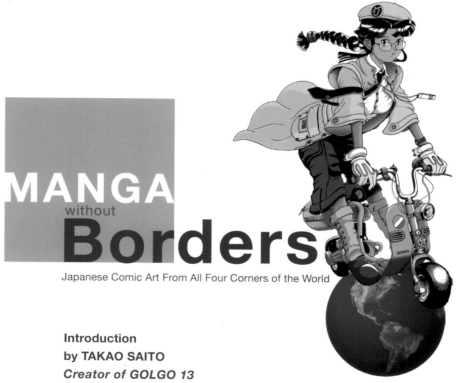

MANGA
without
Borders

Japanese Comic Art From All Four Corners of the World

Introduction
by TAKAO SAITO
Creator of GOLGO 13

MANGA UNIVERSITY PRESENTS ... MANGA WITHOUT BORDERS
Japanese Comic Art From All Four Corners of the World

Published by Manga University under the auspices of Japanime Co. Ltd.,
3-31-18 Nishi-Kawaguchi, Kawaguchi-shi, Saitama-ken 332–0021, Japan.

www.mangauniversity.com

Editor: Glenn Kardy
Designer: Shinobu Sendai

Special thanks to Edward Mazza

First edition, May 2006

ISBN-13: 978-4-921205-05-8
ISBN-10: 4-921205-05-1

06 07 08 09 10   10 9 8 7 6 5 4 3 2 1

Printed in China

FEATURED ARTISTS

INTRODUCTION

by **TAKAO SAITO**
Creator of *Golgo 13*

At first glance, the drawings in this book seem no different than countless other manga illustrations that have come from Japan. All the characters have big eyes. The colors are bright, the lines bold. There are adorable animals and bad-ass mecha. And the girls? Wow!

But I invite you to take a closer look. Notice the high Western nose of the ninja on page 11? How about the African flourish of the headdress worn by the princess on page 33? Or the Nordic features of the kimono-clad beauty on page 17?

These illustrations were created by some of the finest amateur and semi-professional comic artists in the world. All of them share a love of manga—and none of them is Japanese.

What you are witnessing is the internationalization of manga. In many ways, this "Japanese" art form has come full circle. The earliest manga drawings, created way back in the 19th century, were actually a hybrid of traditional Japanese *ukiyo-e* (woodblock prints) and Western-style comic art.

That trend continued as the postwar generation of Japanese artists and storytellers (myself included), influenced by the imported Hollywood movies and translated *amekomi* (American comics) with which we had grown up, began creating our own manga.

Today, manga has become an international phenomenon, and now it is foreign artists who are being influenced by our techniques. Yet at the same time, they infuse manga with elements of their own unique cultures, thus creating a hybrid of the hybrid.

I encourage you again to take a closer look. Study these illustrations carefully. Analyze them. Critique them. Learn from them. Witness the cultural contributions that artists across the globe are making to the Japanese comic art form. Enter the brave new world of manga without borders.

さいとう・たかを

Takao Saito
Tokyo, April 2006

Australia

Lynda Mills

<u>ALL THE RIGHT MOVES</u>

We kick things off with a vision
of the future from Down Under.
This lithe creature looks as though
she'd be just as comfortable
doing battle in the Outback
as she would be fighting cyborgs
on the streets of Tokyo.
Spiderwoman, eat your heart out.

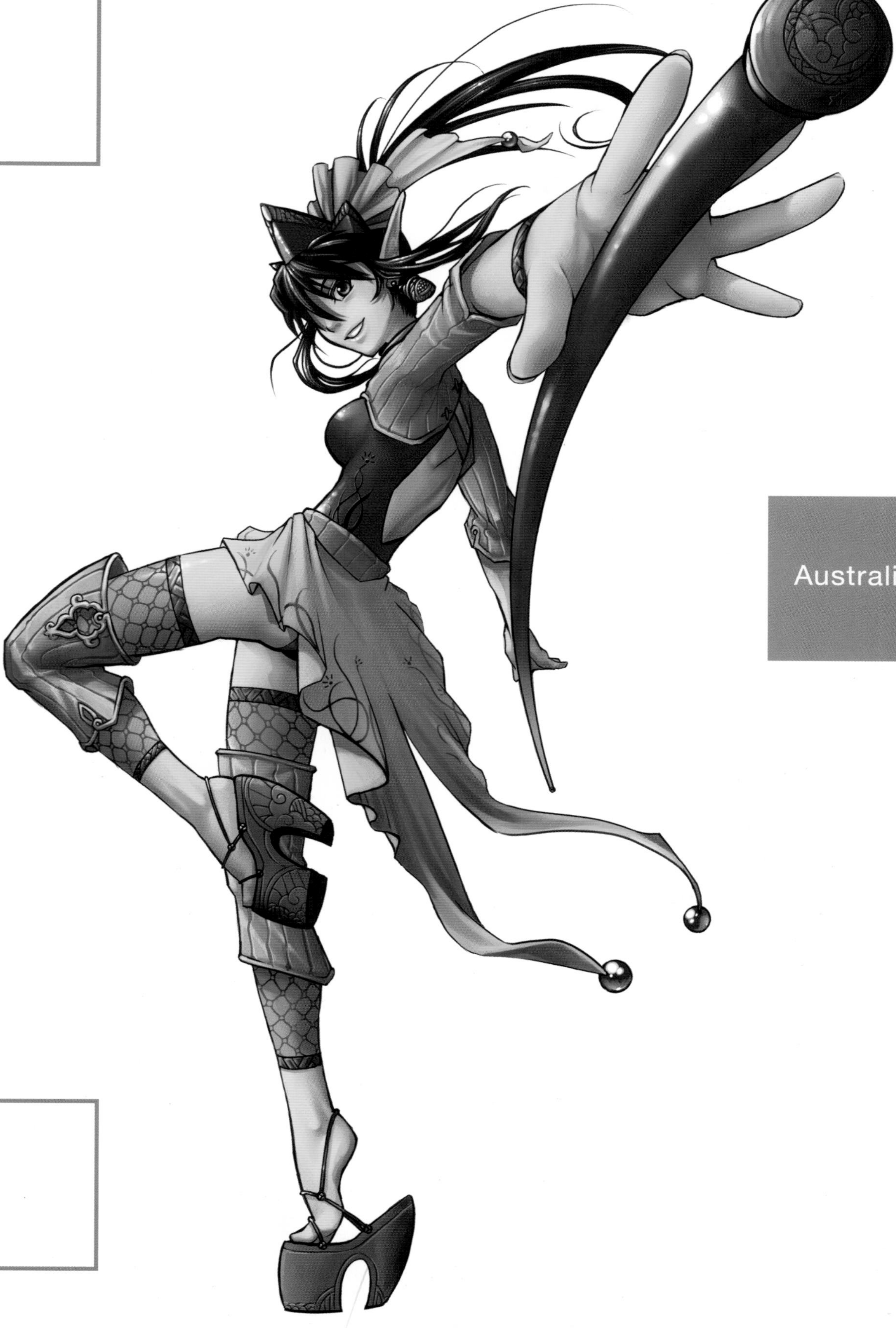

Australia

Hungary

Biro Petra

SEND IN THE CLOWN

Old World influences abound

in this neo-manga rendition

of a classic French pierrot.

The clothes are decidedly European,

but the stunning Japanesque eyes

offer us a cherished glimpse

into the character's anime aspirations.

Hungary

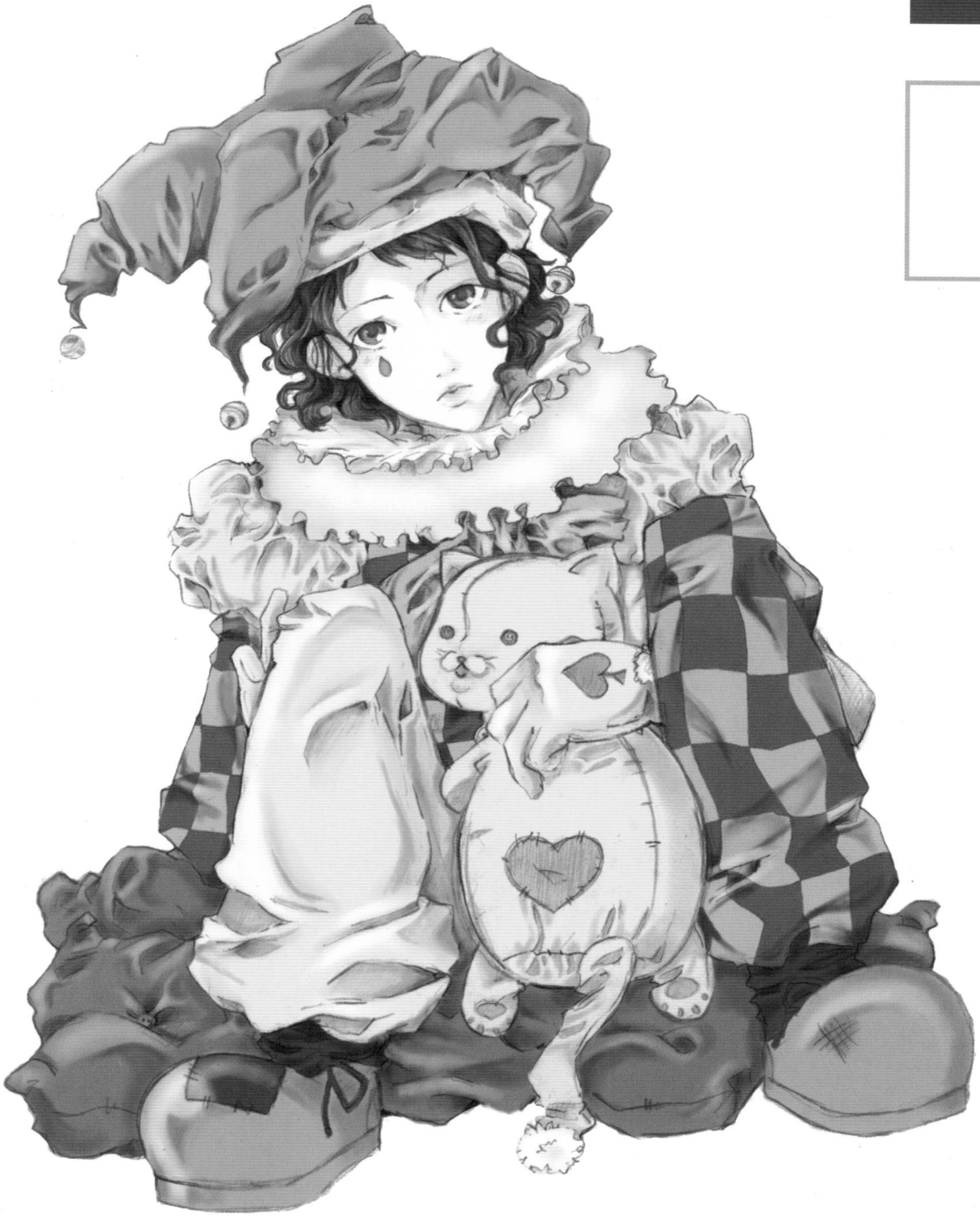

Canada
Janet Cheung

NINJA OF THE NORTH

A genuine warrior babe
with attitude to spare.
Take one look at her face
and you know she's deadly
anywhere on the globe,
from Osaka to Ottawa.

Canada

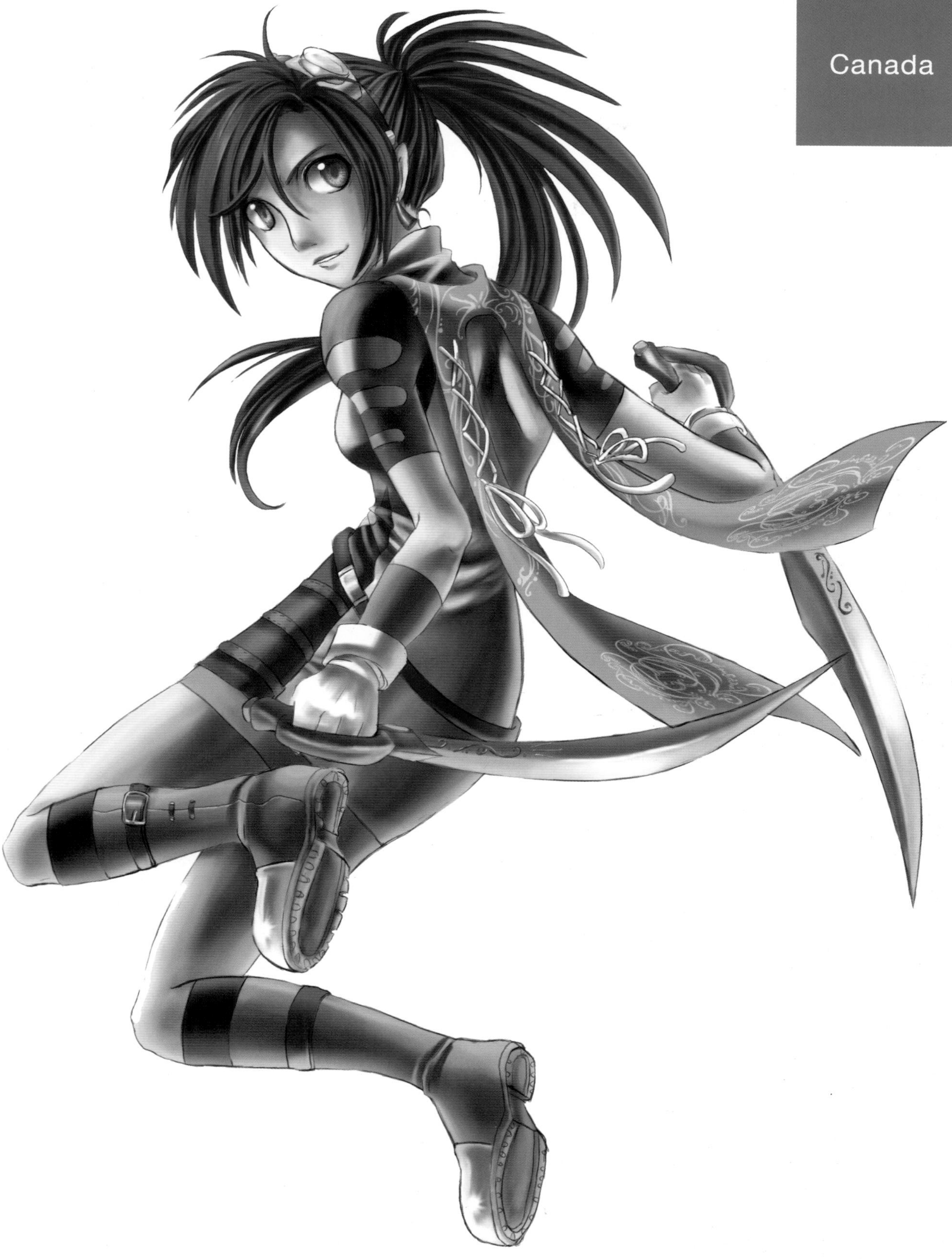

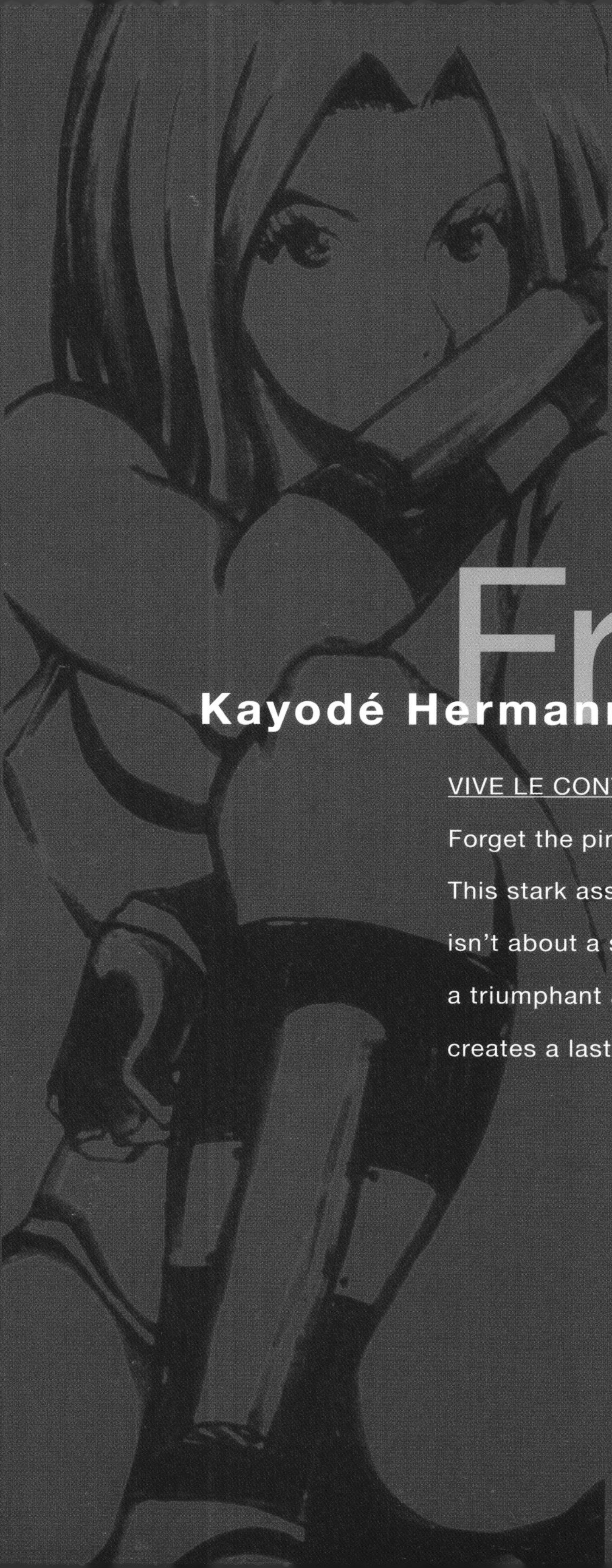

France

Kayodé Hermann

VIVE LE CONTRAST

Forget the pink hair, forget the blue eyes. This stark assassin proves that manga isn't about a splash of color and flash; a triumphant arc of black ink on paper creates a lasting image of a femme fatale.

France

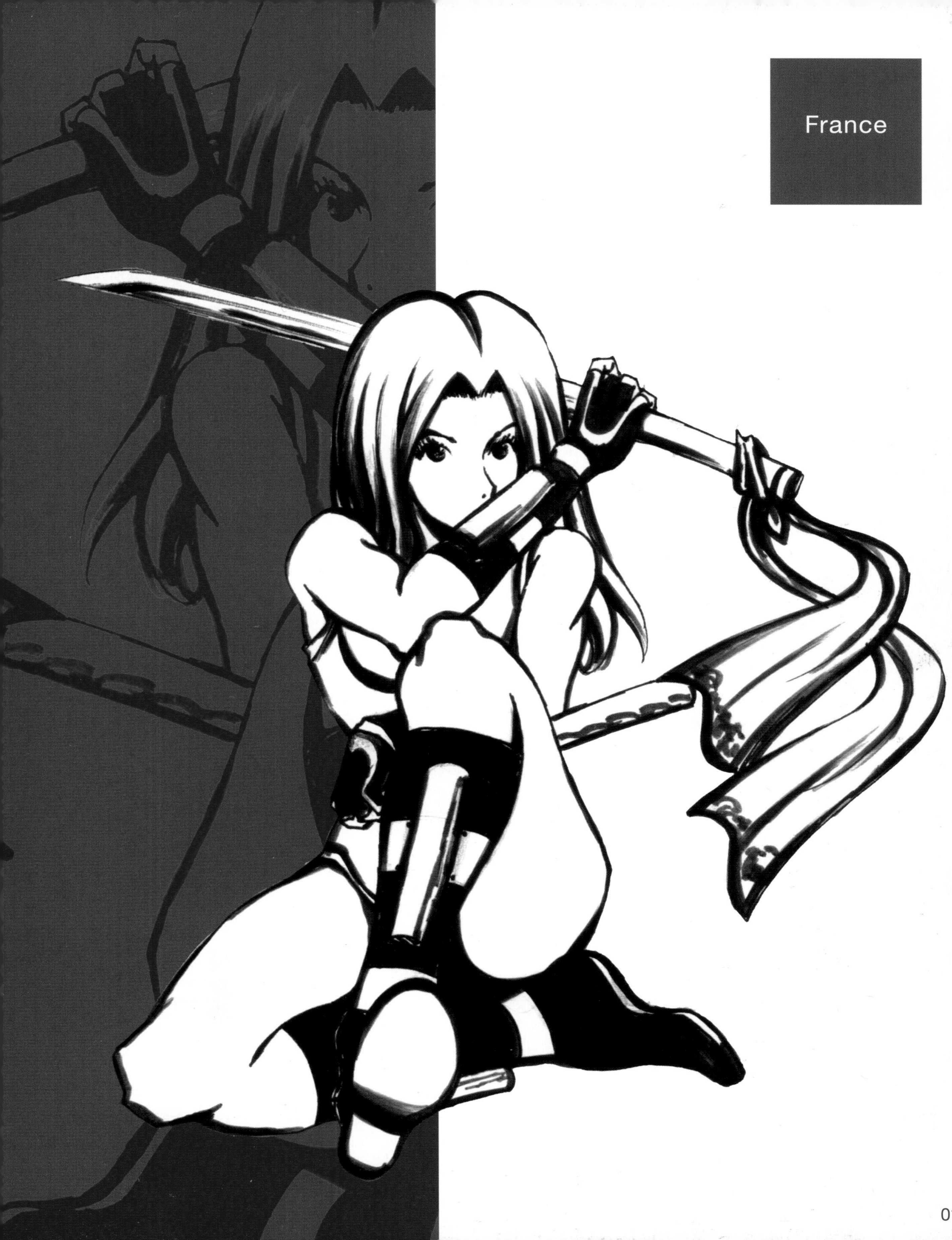

Sweden

Jennie Halen

FLOWING FANTASY

She's a European woman

with elven features straight

from Western fantasy tales.

But there's no denying

the manga twist on her;

she would blend perfectly

into the latest Japanese creations.

Sweden

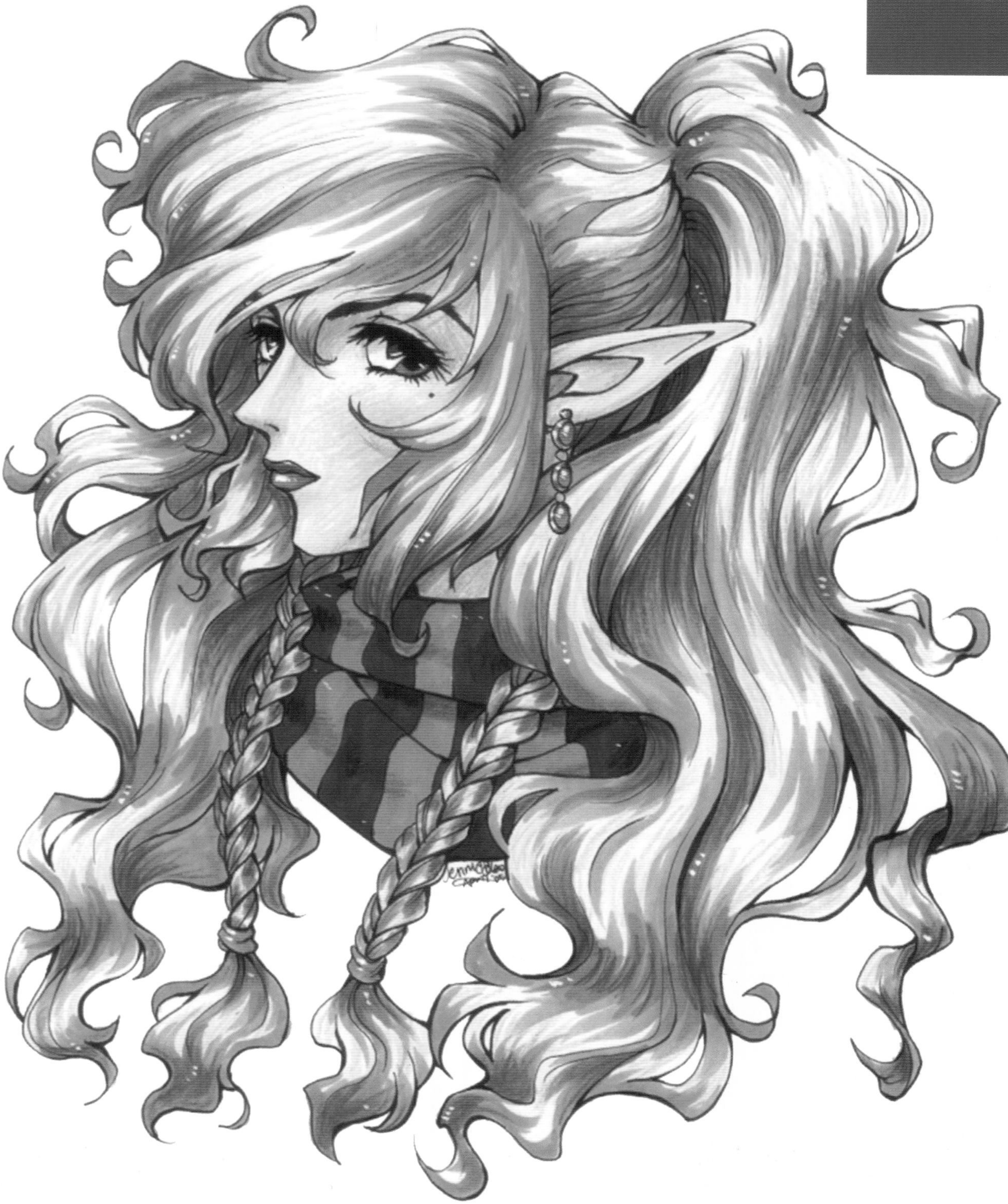

Norway

Øyvind Sørøy

NORWEGIAN WOOD

A clear cross between
Northern Europe and Japan
combines in classic beauty.
The engravings on the pen
show an obvious flair for style
and a craftman's love of art.

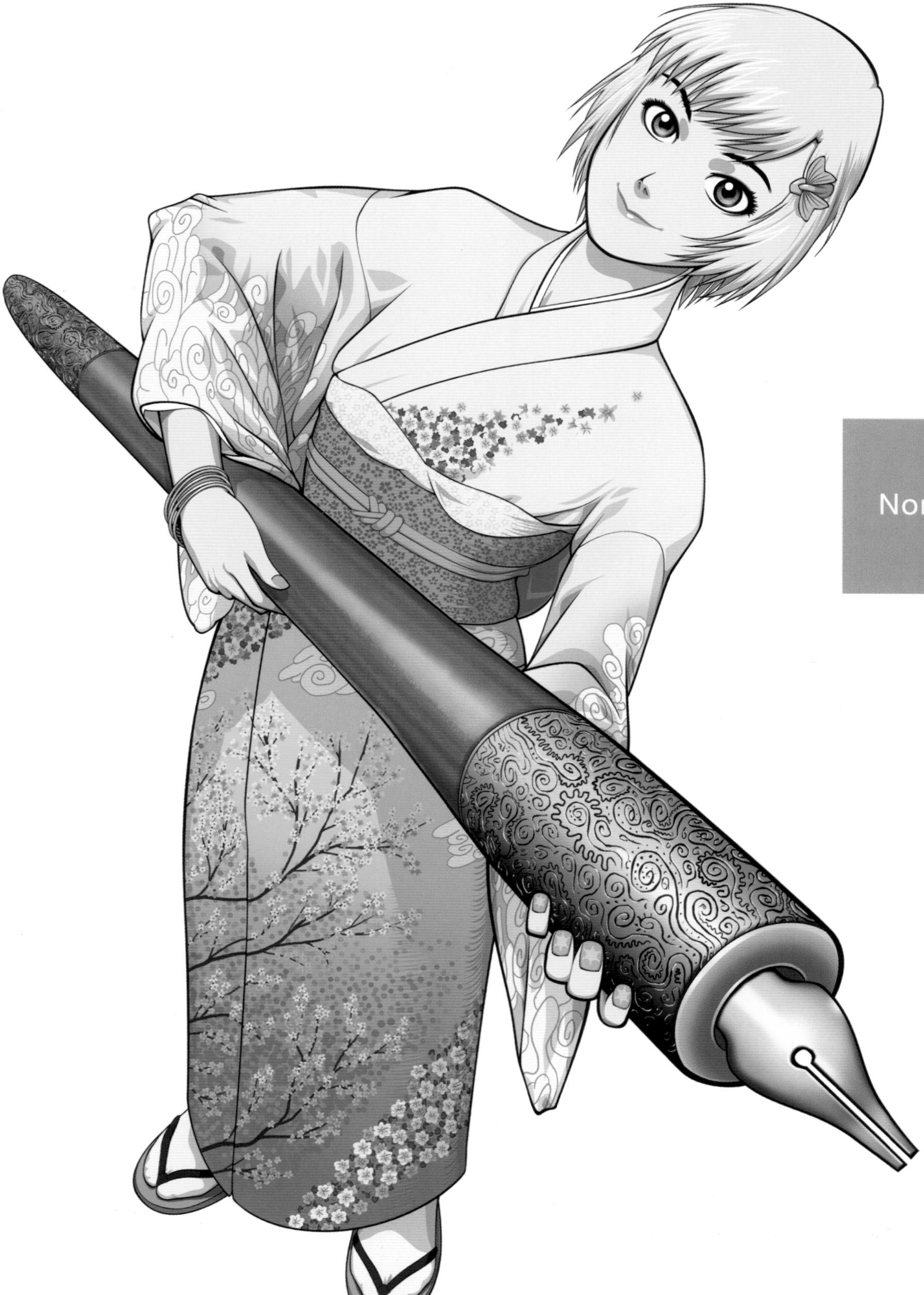

Norway

Australia

Craig Judd

<u>THINK PINK</u>

This manga gal's gone hip hop.

Just like mashups are all the rage

in the world of music, our gal here

is a trendy mashup all her own.

Her style is off the hippest streets;

the technique is anime all the way.

Australia

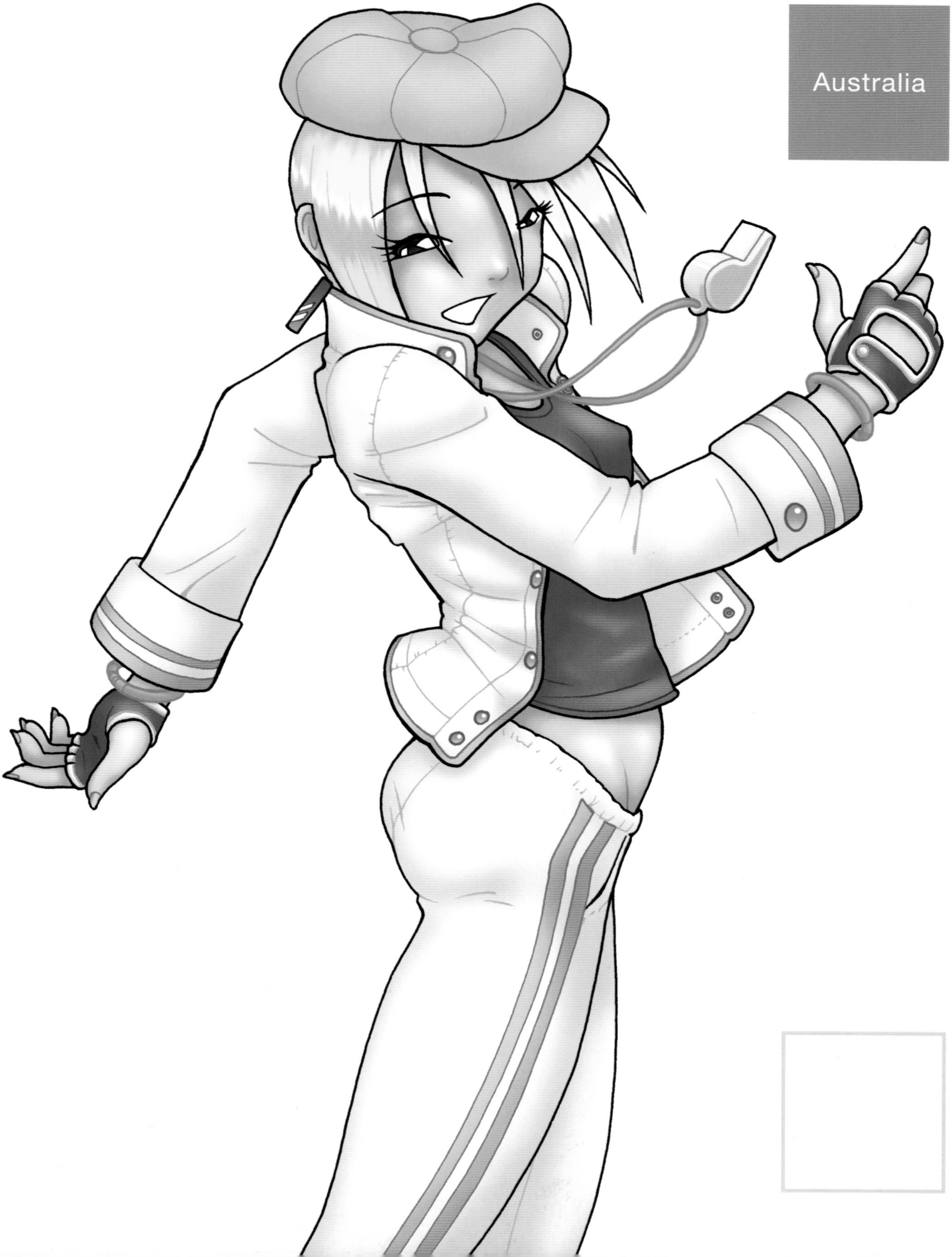

Philippines

Jade Ong

SHE'S GOT GAME

Who says manga is only about

giant robots and schoolgirls?

With a backhand that would make

Anna Kournikova green with envy,

this sassy athlete proves that

jocks have a place in comics too.

Philippines

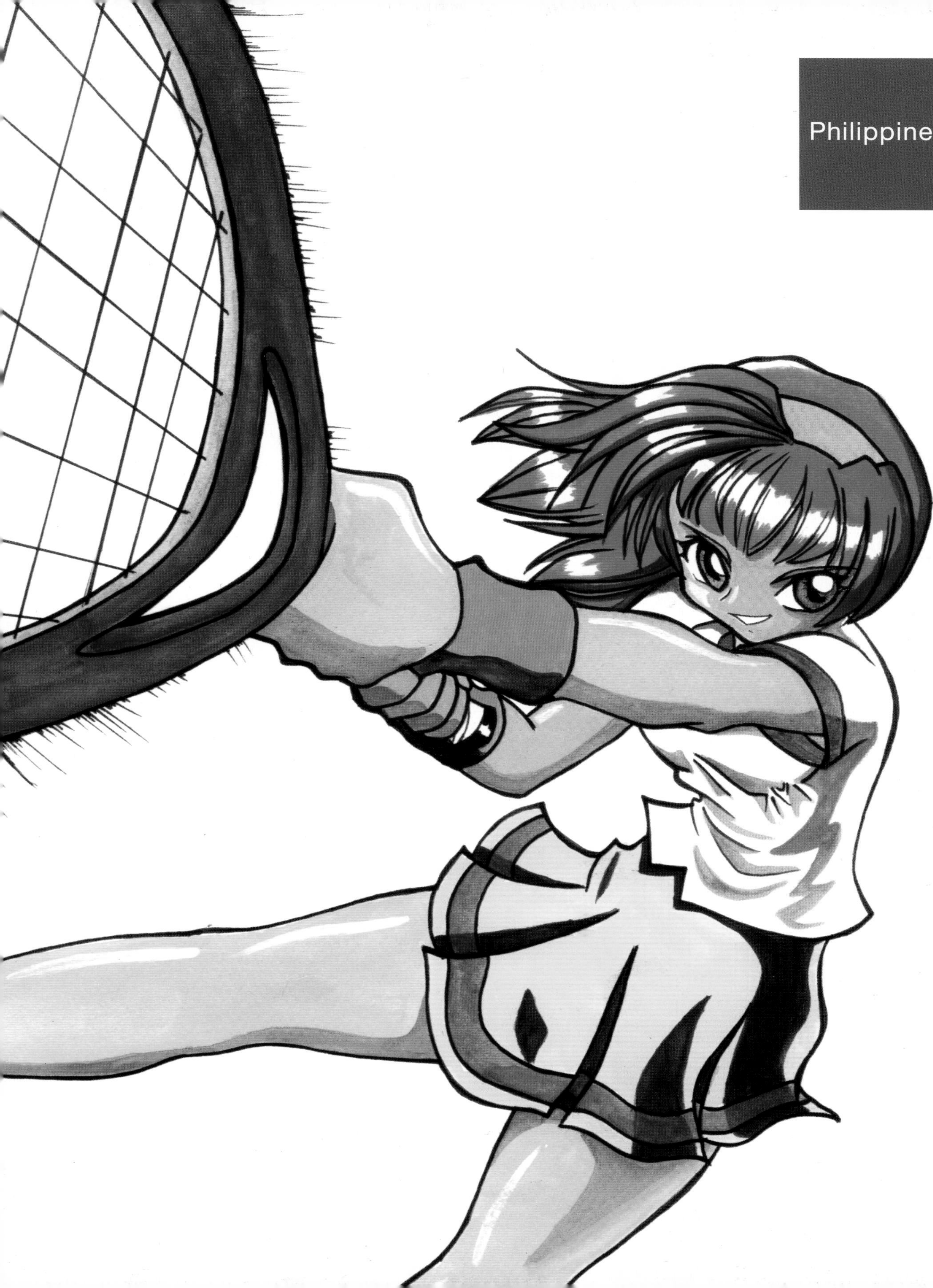

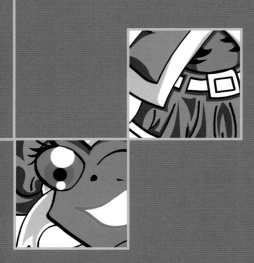

The United States of America

Sandy Qadamani

FROGGY FLAIR

This little frog doesn't need a kiss;

it's already an aristocratic amphibian.

Note the creative spin on period clothes

and the stylish cap topped with a tuff.

Never have webbed feet looked so good!

USA

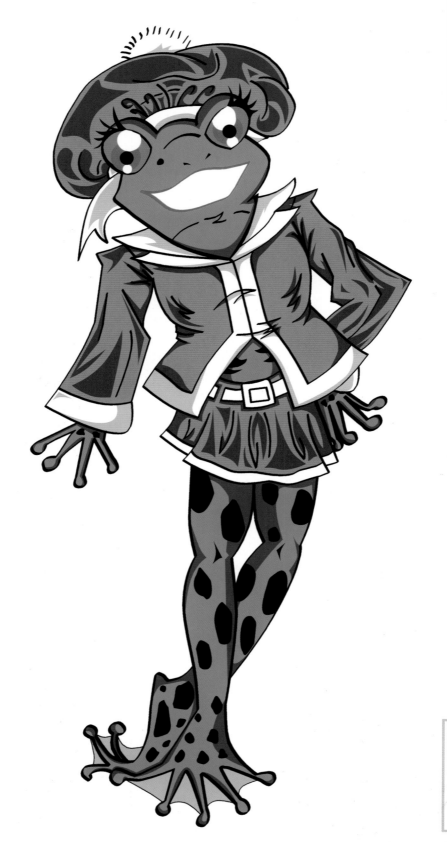

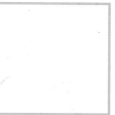

The
Netherlands

Sunny Sunil Sital

BAKA BALL

A rough day on the playground

or a young tough ready to rumble.

We know one thing for sure:

He's crazy and cool

but definitely nobody's fool!

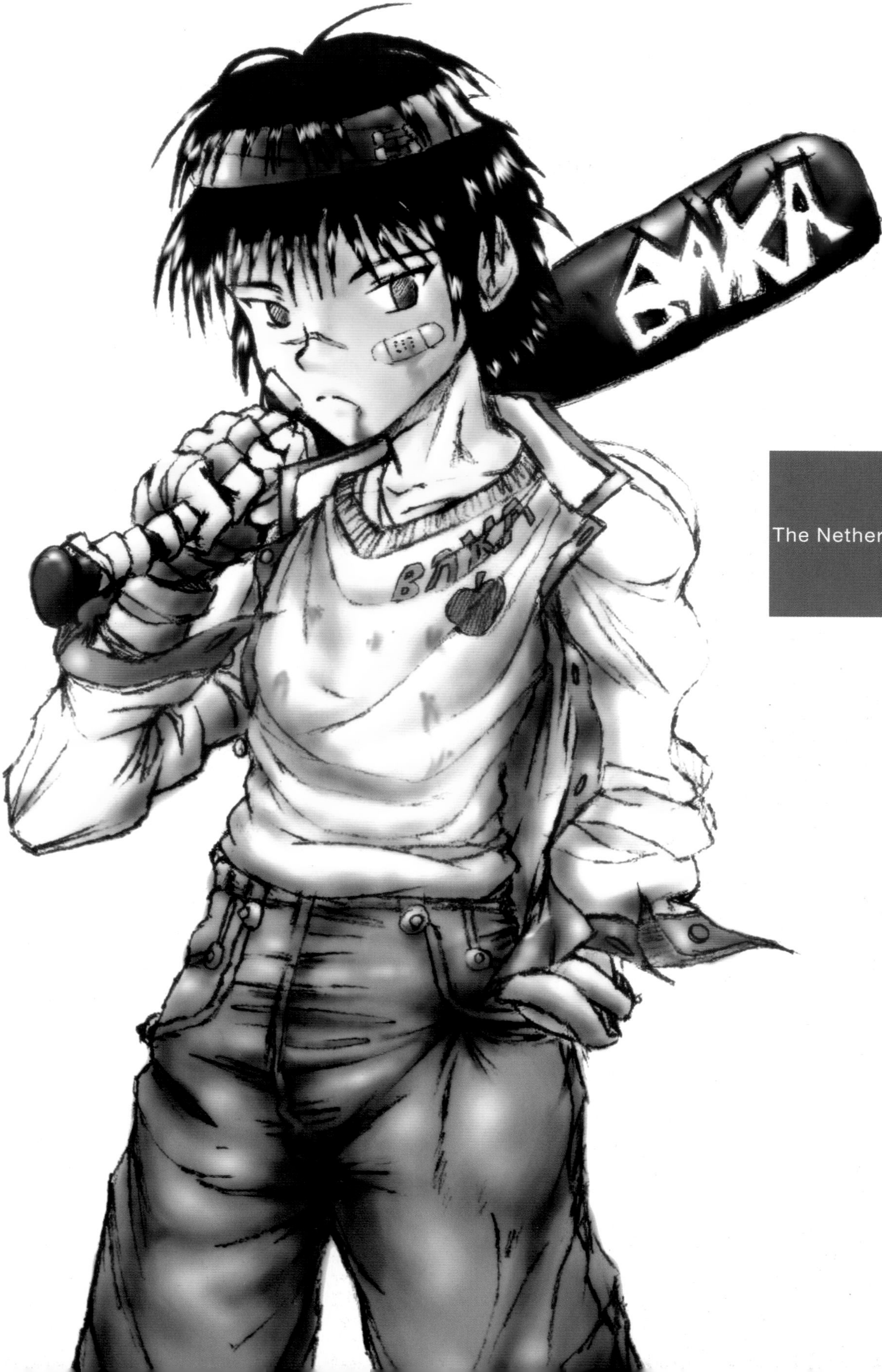
BAKA

The Netherlands

The United States of America

Jamal Jorif

<u>BOY, AHOY!</u>

He may not exactly be Popeye,

and his anchor-shaped earrings

will definitely turn some heads,

but this maritime angel knows

pretty little sailor suits

aren't just for Japanese schoolgirls.

USA

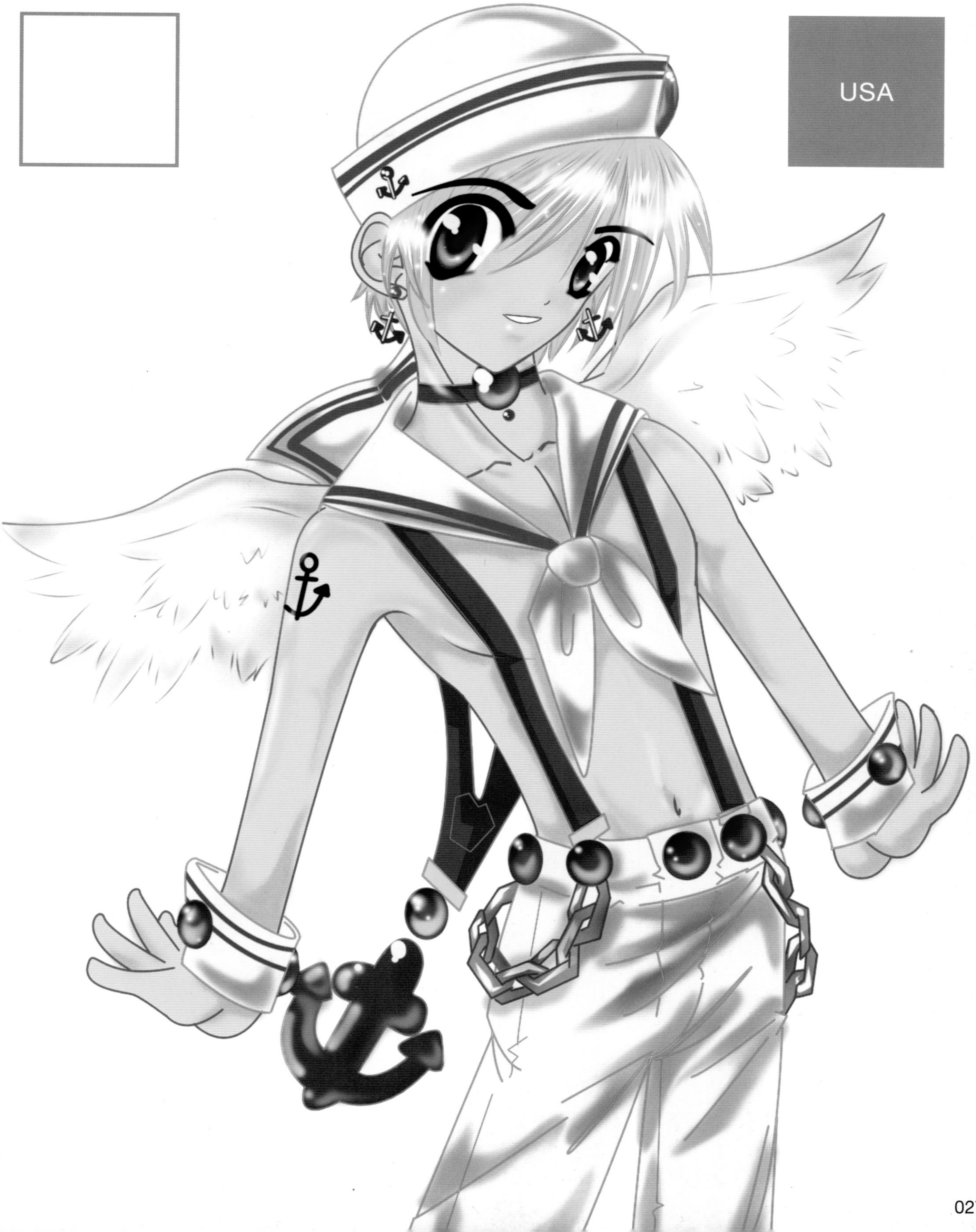

Poland

Le Thi Minh Khuyen

THE LITTLE WITCH

With a wink and a whisper,

she knows something you don't.

With her trusty cat looking on

and a broom at the ready,

she has all that she needs

to put a spell on you.

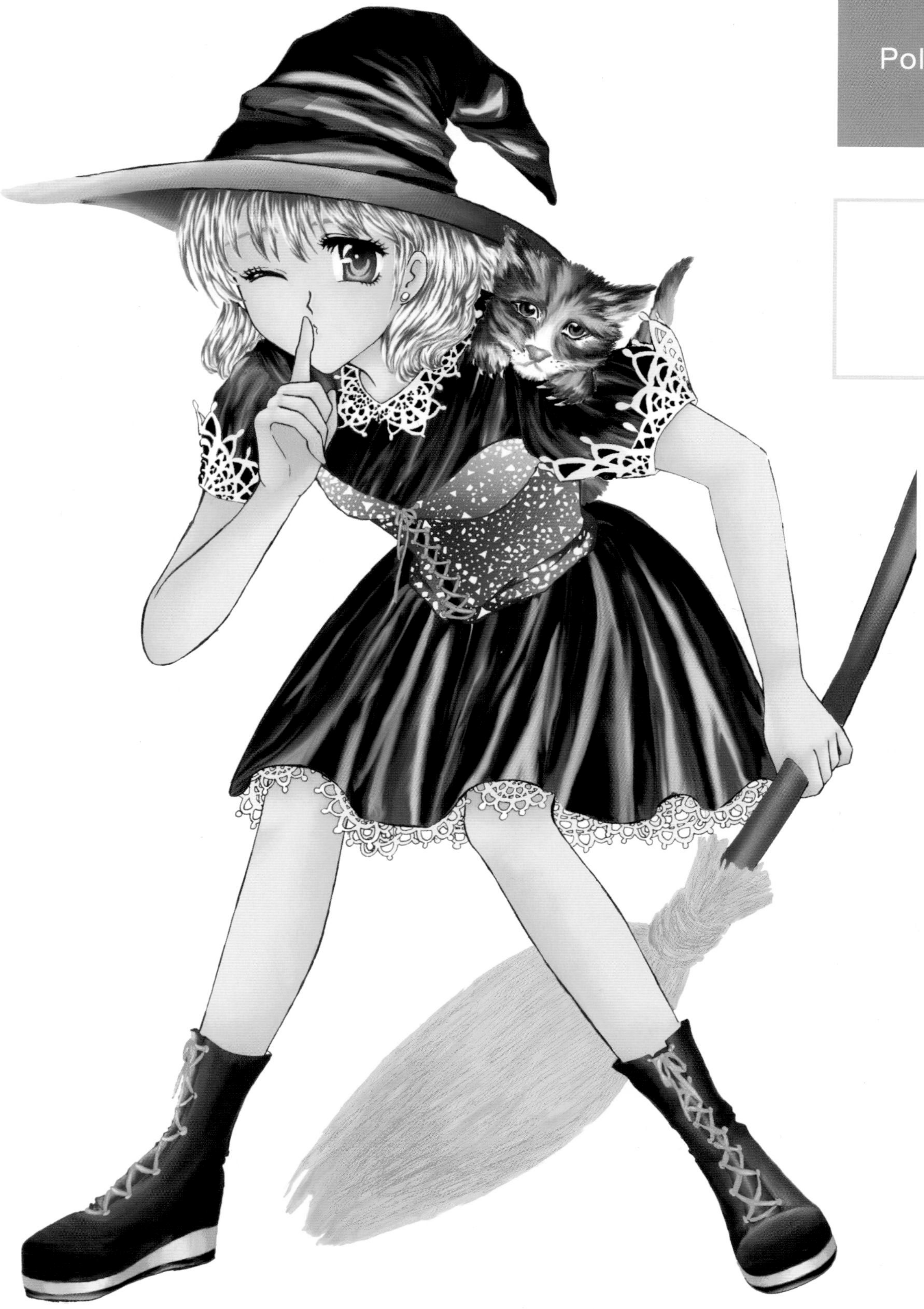

Poland

United Kingdom

Rachael Gregg-Smythe

BEAUTY AND THE BRAIDS

Curves like these

are seldom seen

in all but the bawdiest

of Japanese manga.

But don't ignore her

just because she's beautiful!

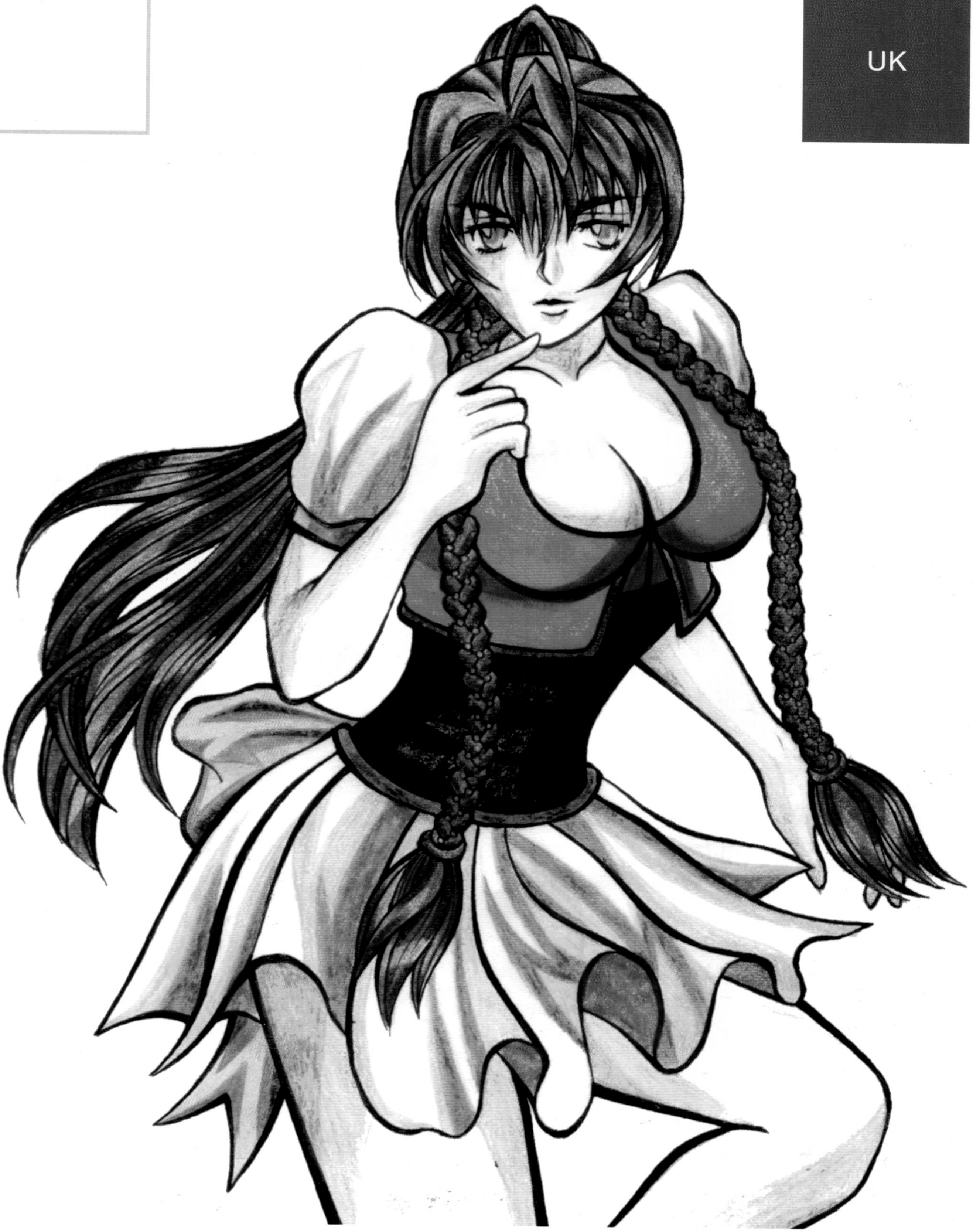

UK

South Africa

Kithue Masu

<u>AFRICAN QUEEN</u>

Here's what happens when

manga meets real royalty.

Her gown commands respect,

the headdress says "Africa"

and the eyes tell us this is manga.

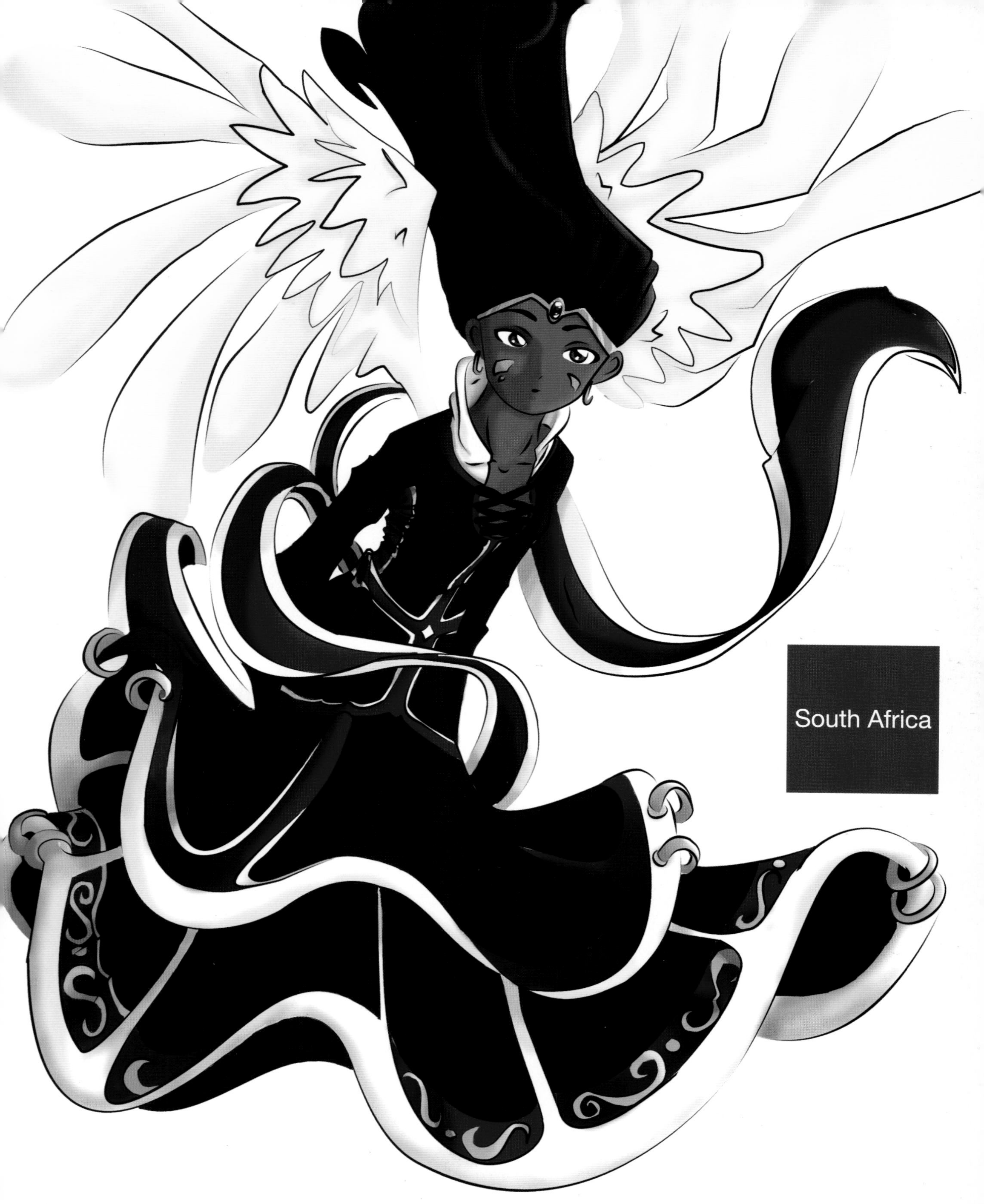

South Africa

Australia

Fiona Chan

<u>PINK POWER</u>

She's prettty in pink,

but don't let that fool you.

The marks on her scabbard

prove she's battle-tested.

This little lass is a perfect fit

for the next installment in the

Sakura Taisen game series.

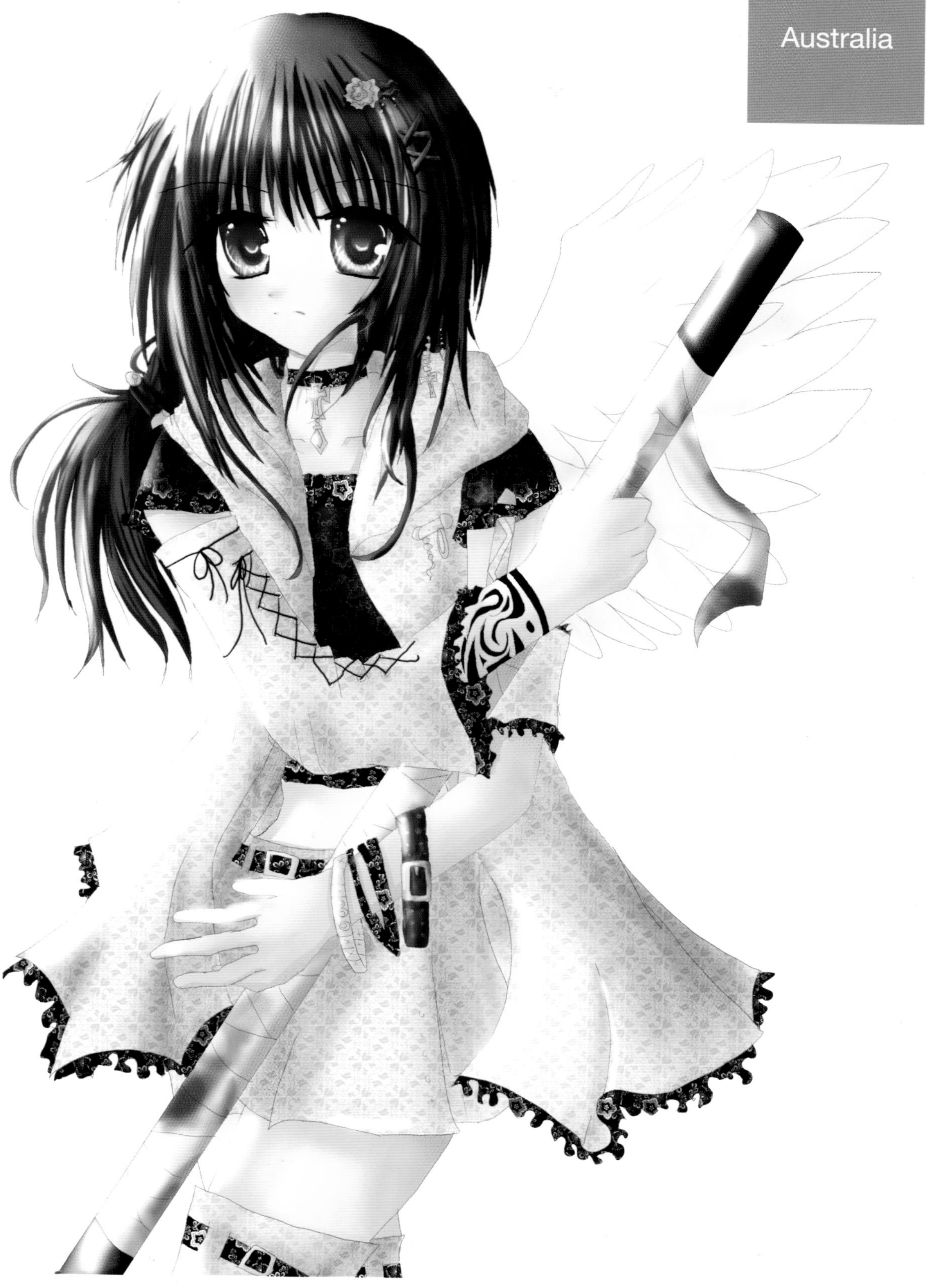

Canada

Ying-Ting Liu

<u>MODERN CLASSIC</u>

Old meets new in this fine work.

A Western beauty with red hair,

green eyes and a tie-dye shirt

shows clear manga influence,

but the pose is timeless.

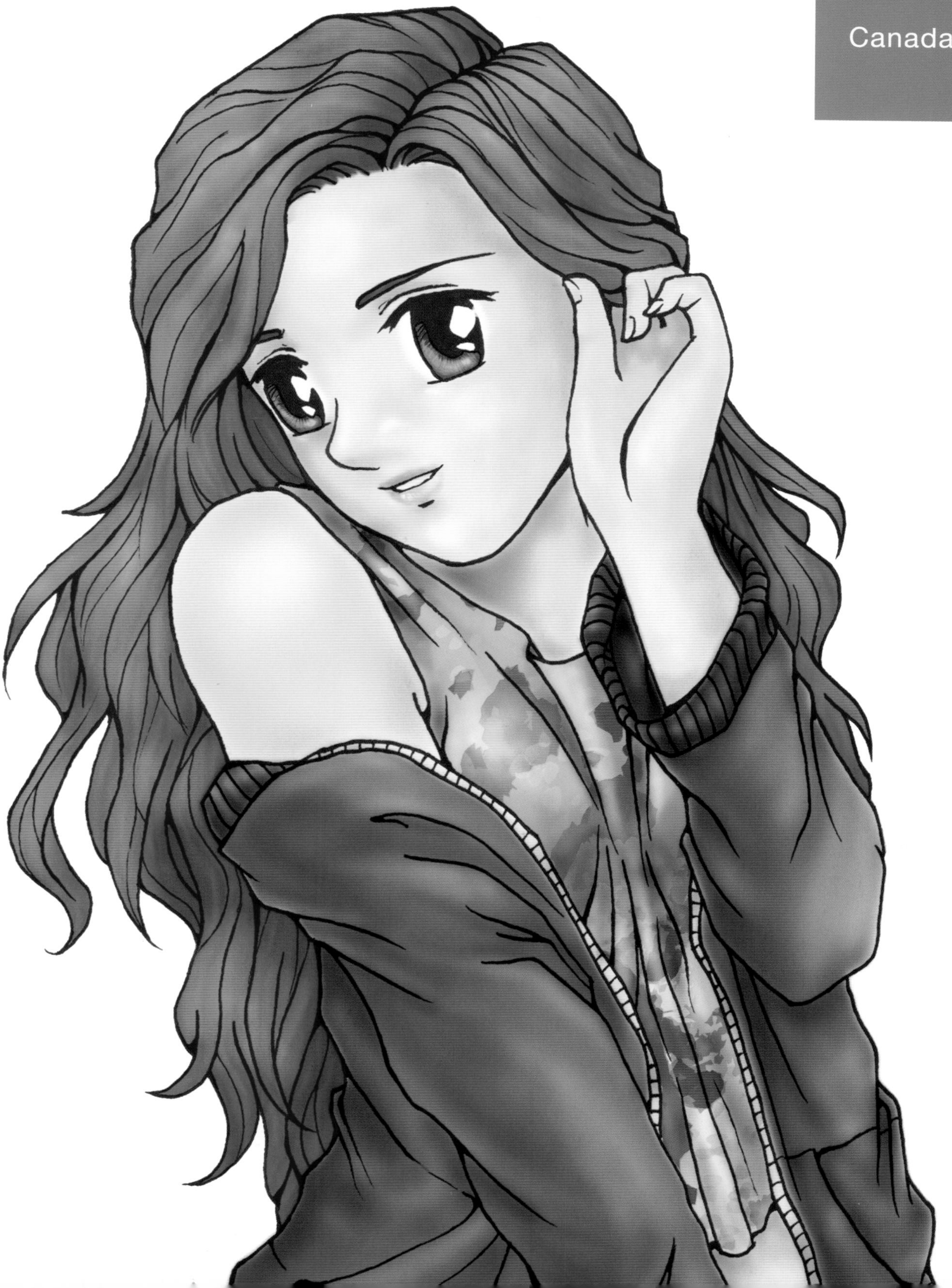

The United States
of America

Stacey Lee Phillips

STAR GAZER

Here's an American girl

through and through.

But don't let the look fool you;

her coy smile suggests

there's something inside.

A joke? A dream? A secret?

USA

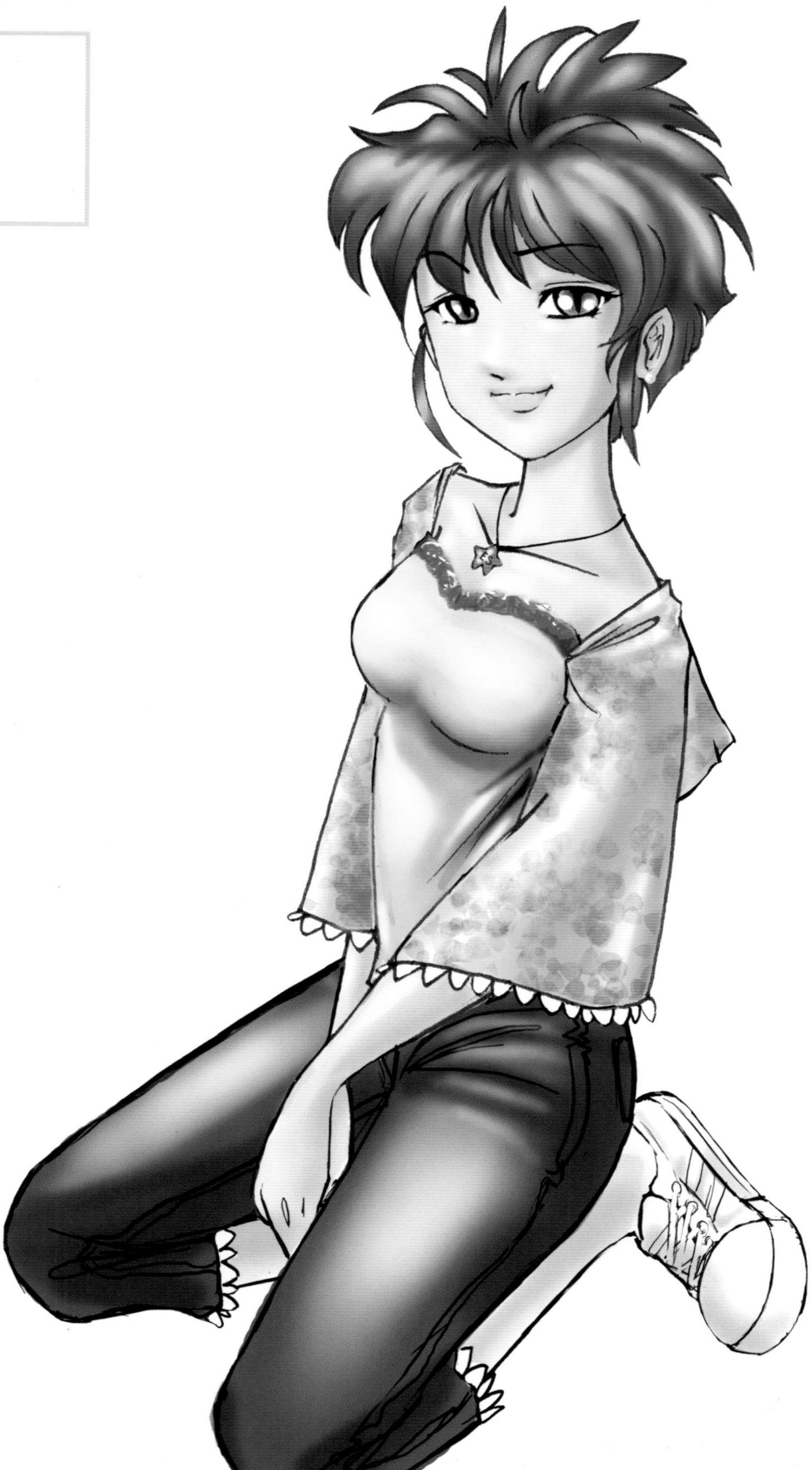

United Kingdom

Justin Telford

<u>TATTOO YOU</u>

Go ahead... make her day!

She's a tough little lady

and she's armed to the teeth.

Yet the pink shoes

and a touch of lace

show the manga girl beneath.

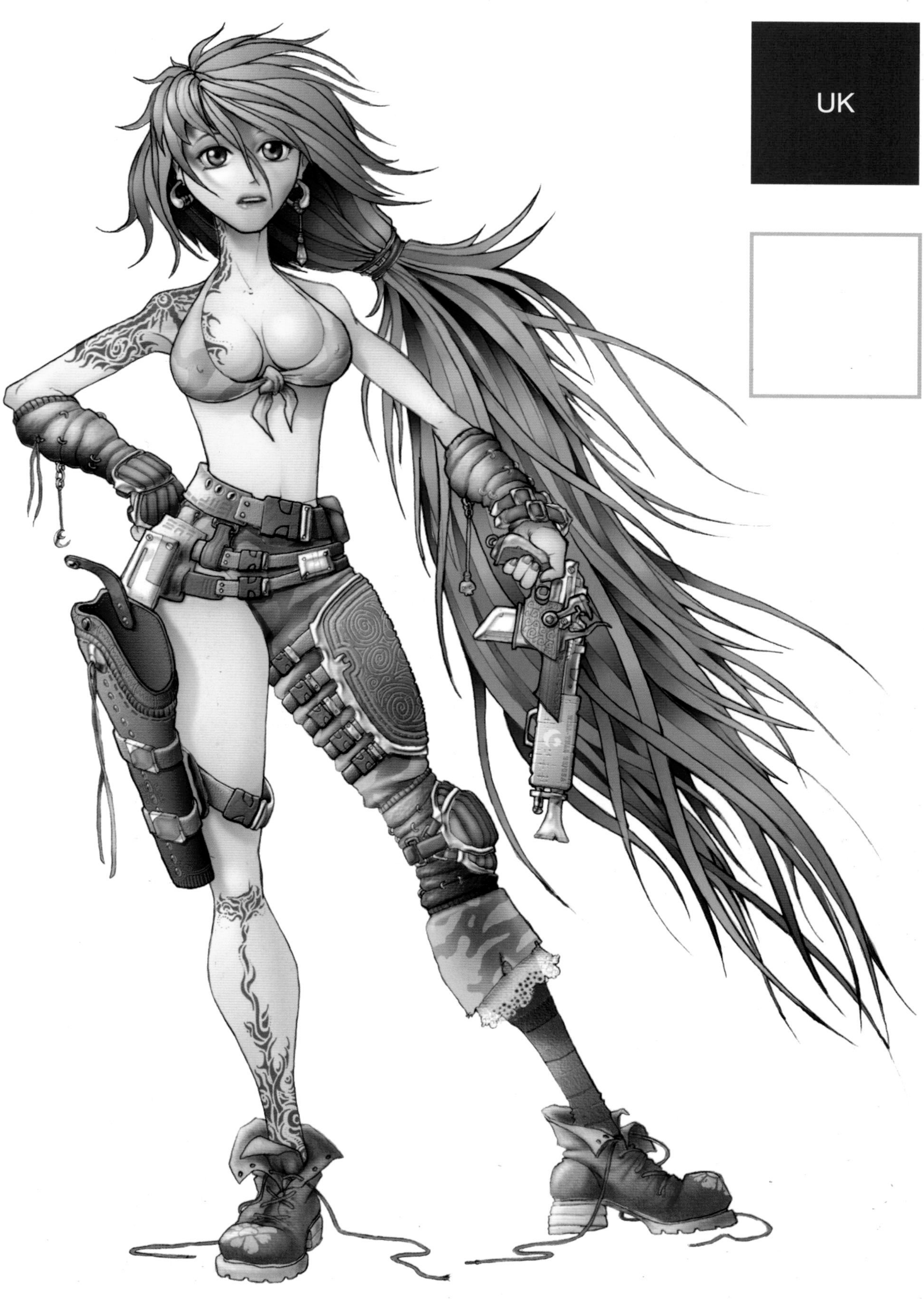

UK

Canada

Holly Rorke

<u>RED ALERT</u>

Shadows create the mystery

of a manga girl clad in crimson.

Note the hint of blue

in her eyes as she peeks

from behind her fiery bangs,

making you pause to wonder:

What's on this girl's mind?

Canada

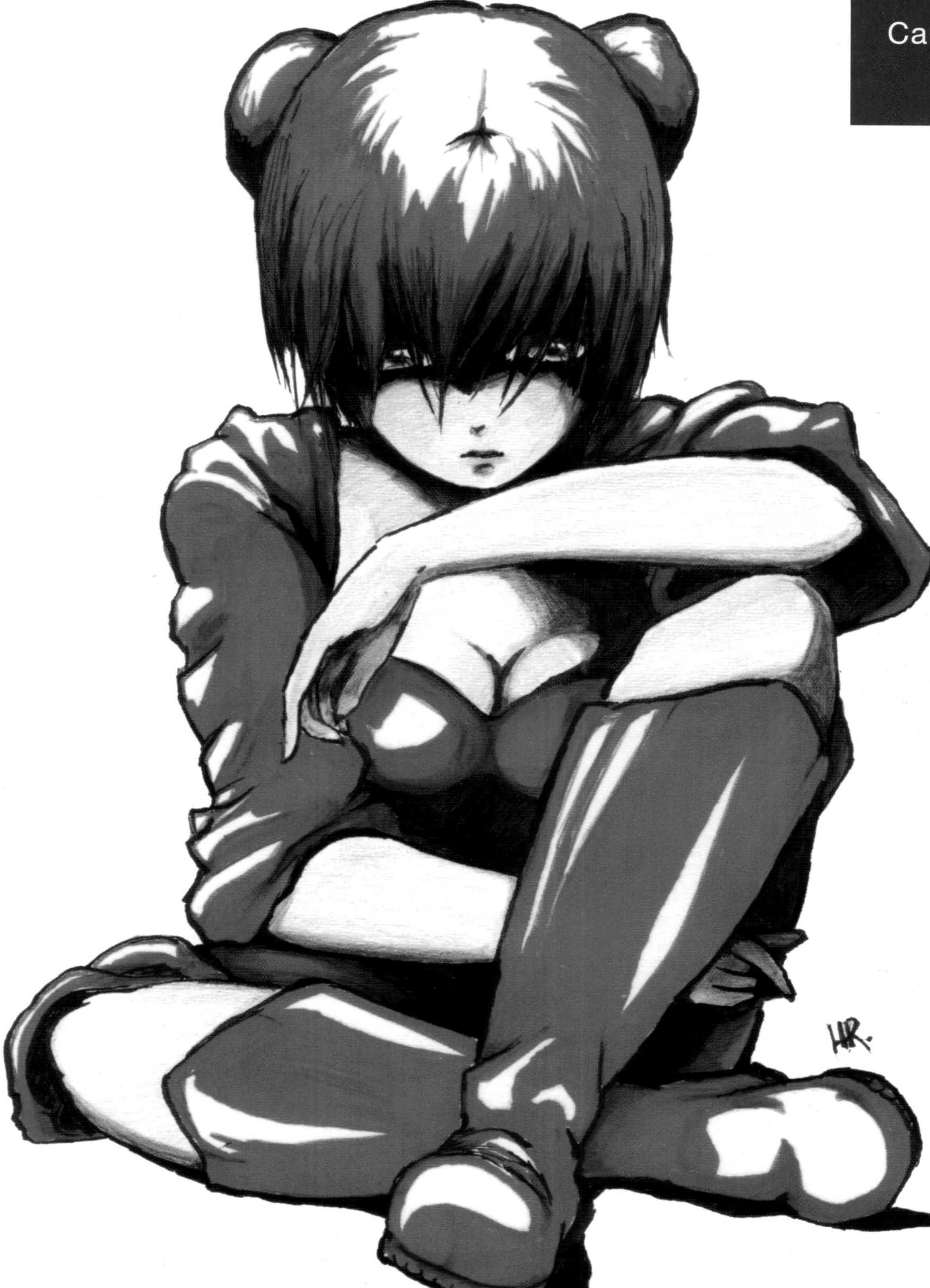
HR.

Holland

Maartje Heere

<u>WILD CHILD</u>

Here's a character

with a real wild streak.

A classic manga marriage

of human and animal.

Her collar matches a piece on her tail;

she's either domesticated, or maybe

she just has a great sense of style.

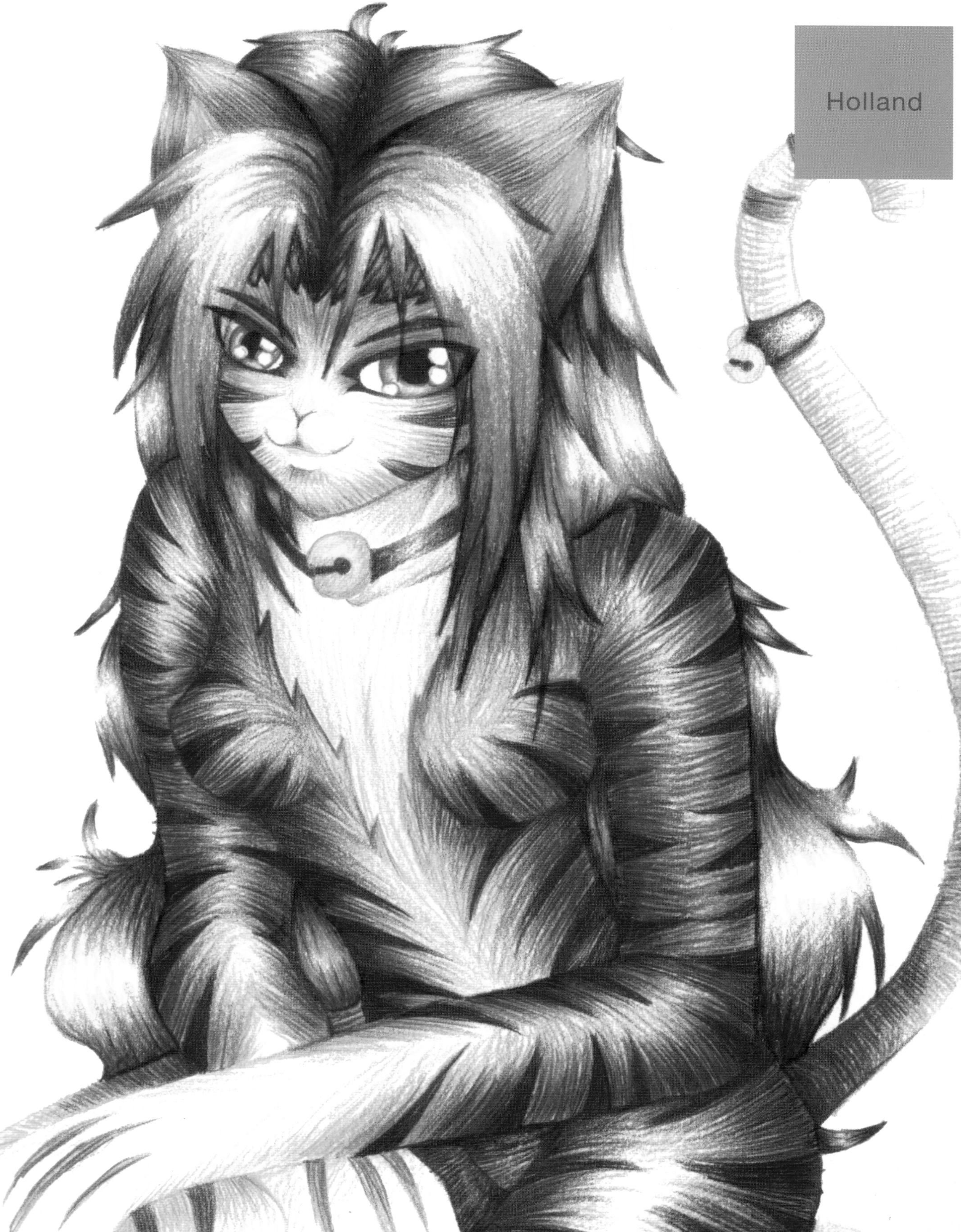
Holland

Canada

Colin Tan

BLUE NOTE

She's the best of both worlds:

A manga girl with Western pizzazz.

Somehow, she manages to turn

blue into a feminine color:

from her eyes to her boots,

there's not a drop of pink around.

Canada

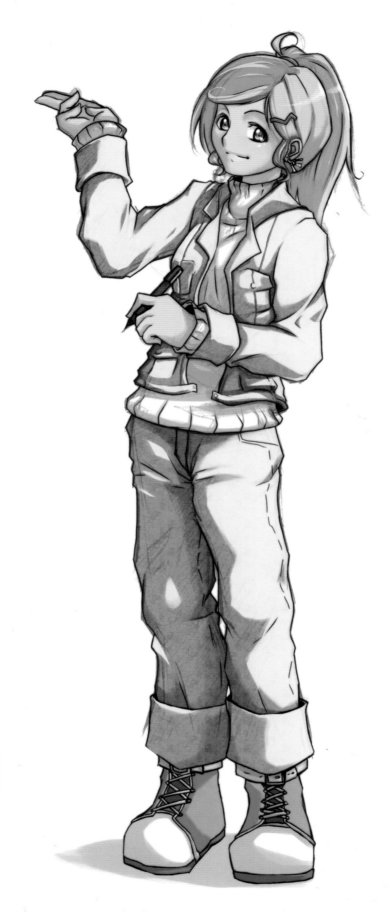

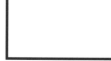

Estonia

Galina Holeneva

<u>TRAVELING LIGHT</u>

Where might she be going,

this lonely neko girl?

Her heart remains

in Northeastern Europe,

but she has hopped aboard a train

that will take her far away

to the magic world of manga.

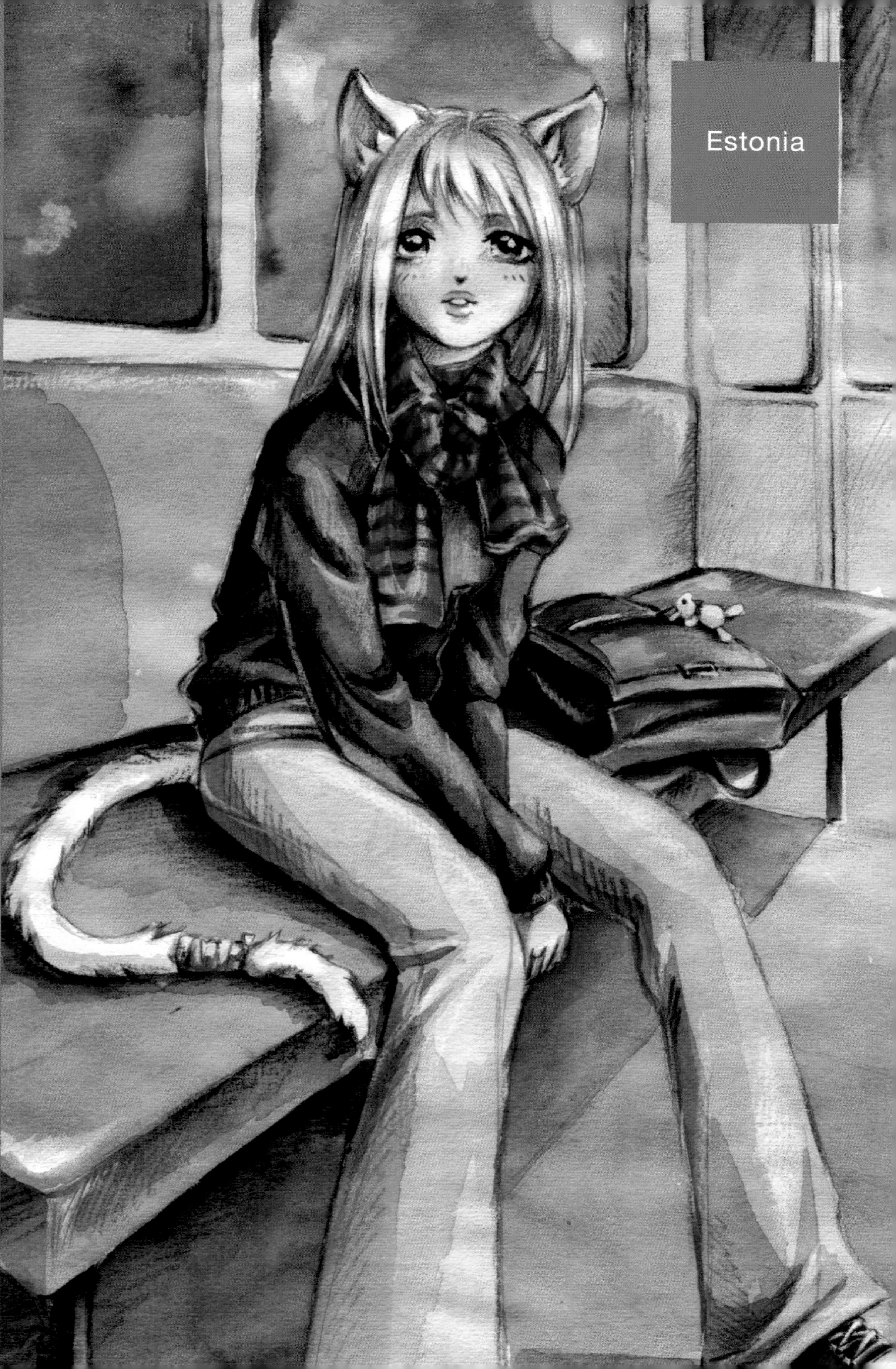
Estonia

South Africa

Hendriaan Janse van Rensburg

CULTURE CLUB

At first this may seem

like a woodblock print.

But look a little closer

for a manga mystery.

She's hiding something

beneath those robes.

South Africa

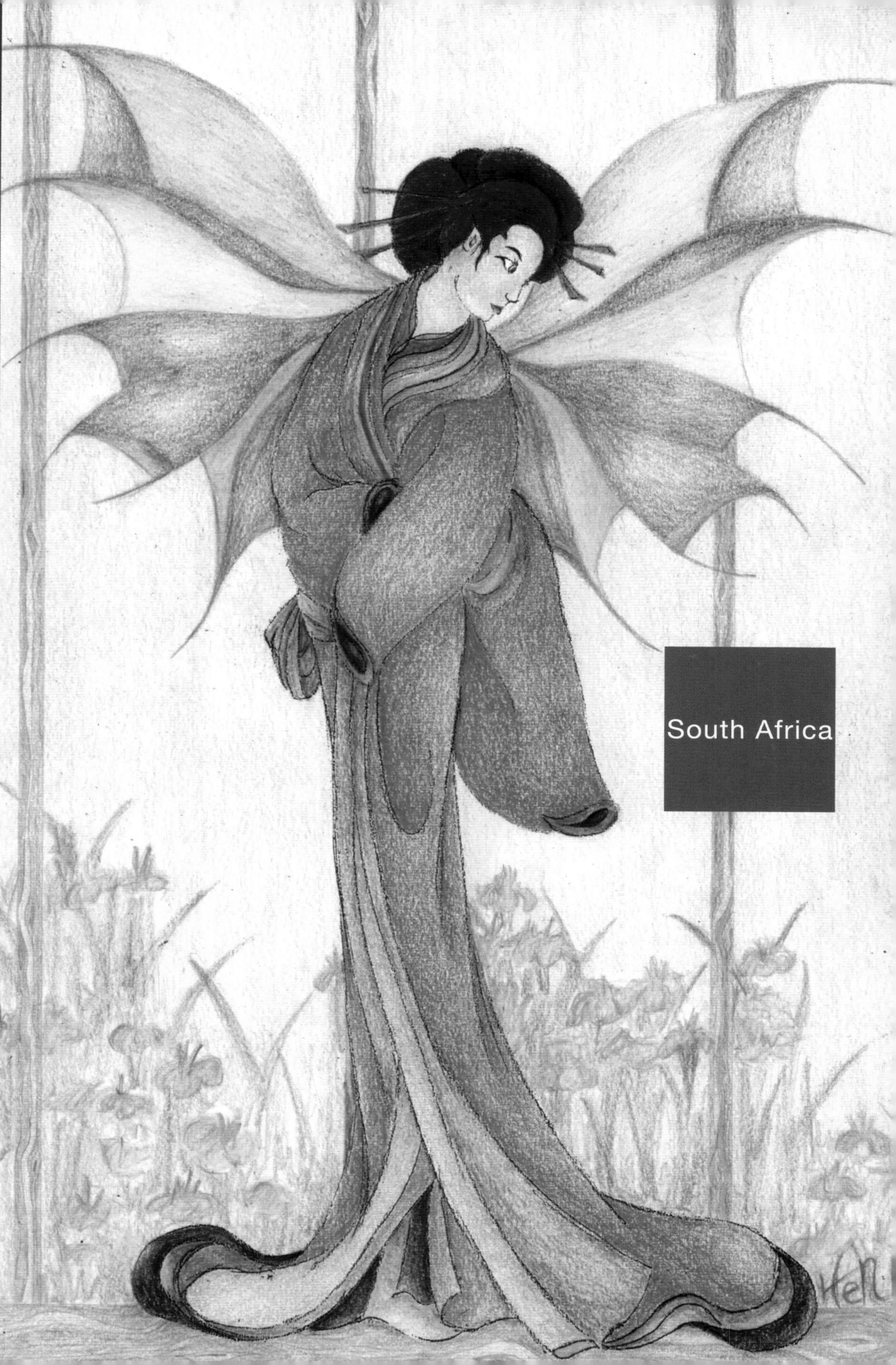

Hungary

Ore Krisztina

FANTASTIC FAIRY

Old World children's tales are filled

with lovely characters such as she.

Modern manga, though,

also has its fair share of sprites.

Our friend here would be

right at home in either.

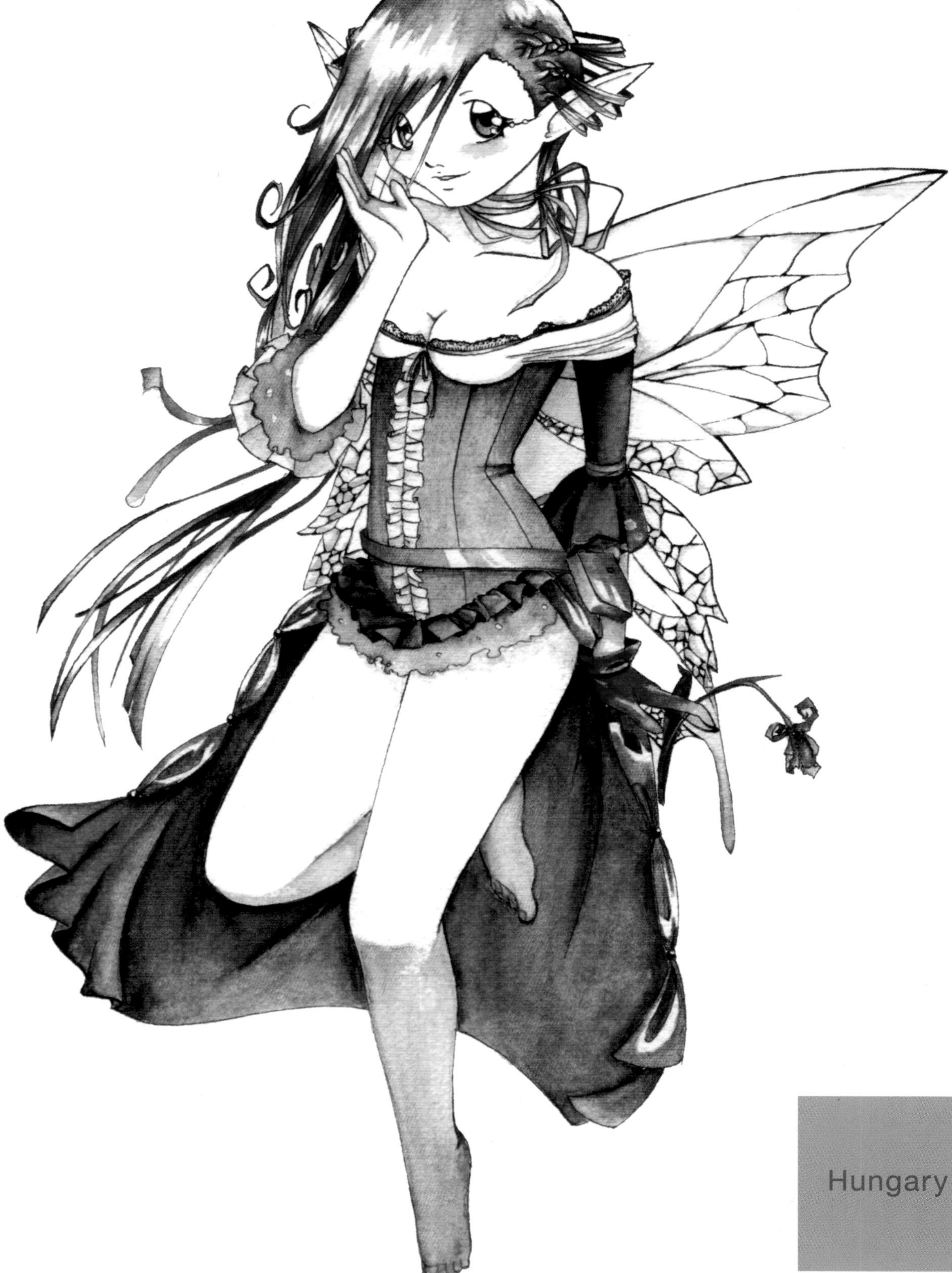

Hungary

France

Stefano Collavini

<u>GOTHIC LOLITA</u>

With her Mona Lisa smile,

innocent manga eyes

and nightmarish garb,

this strange little girl

is a real riddle.

Can you break her code?

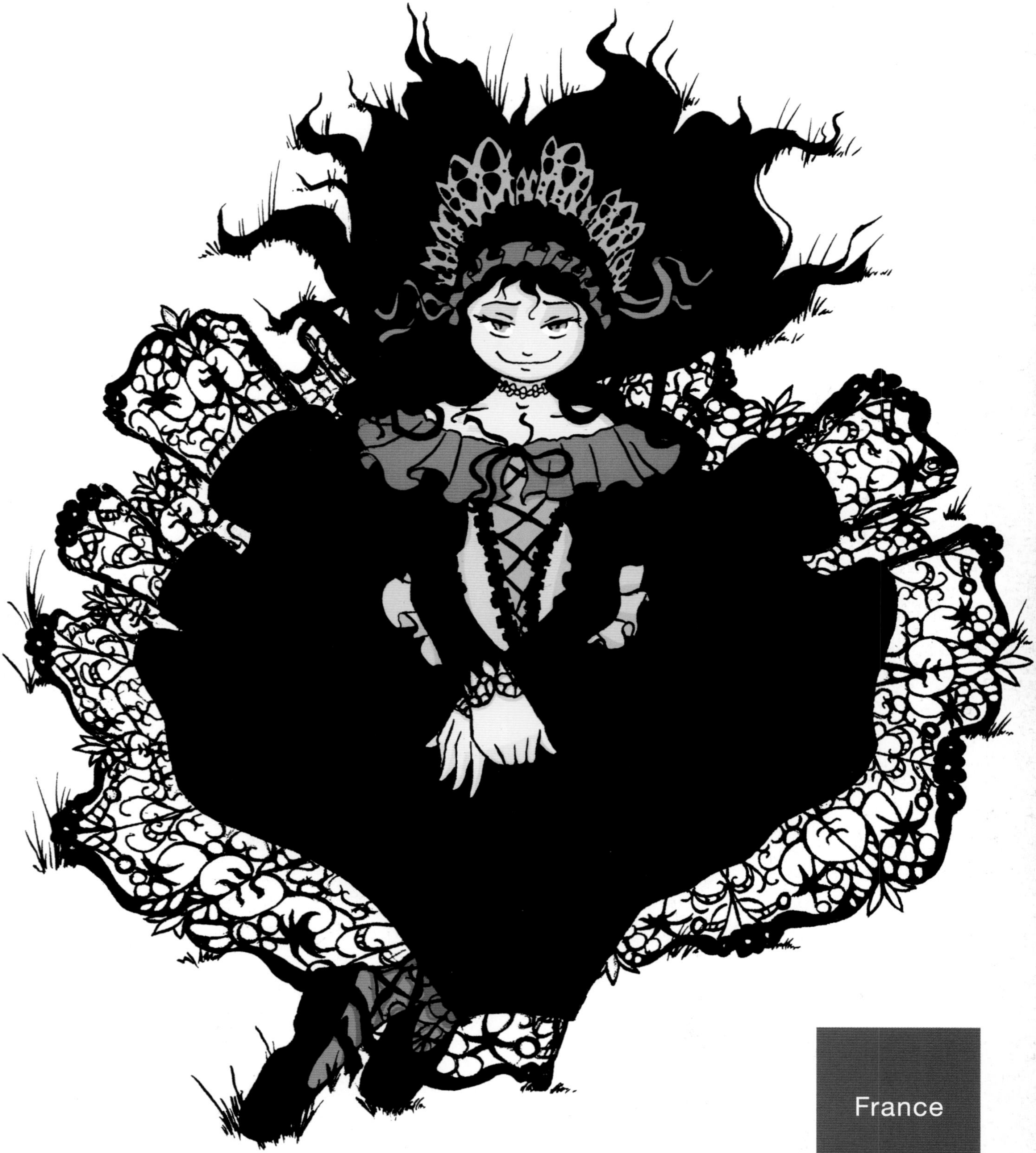

France

Canada

Sarah VanDijk

<u>EN GARDE</u>

Samurai warriors, beware!
You have met your match
in this mighty swordsman.
He has come from the North
to do battle in the East,
mixing medieval techniques
with Japanese traditions.

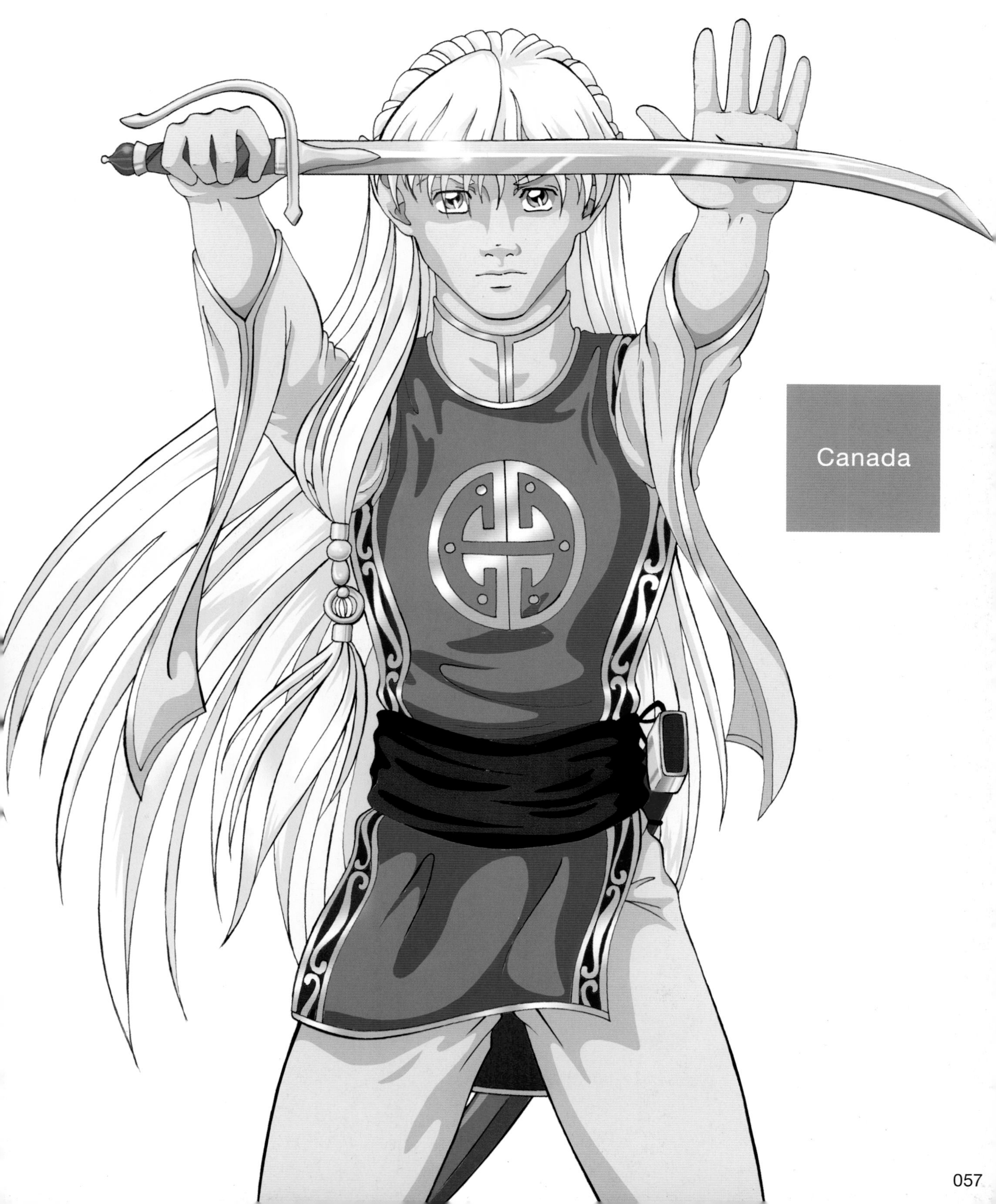

Canada

Australia

David Li

<u>READY TO RUMBLE</u>

With a gal like this keeping watch,

the universe is safe from monsters.

The weapons and armor are recognizable

to manga fans around the world

as classic elements of mecha chic.

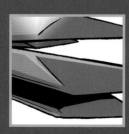

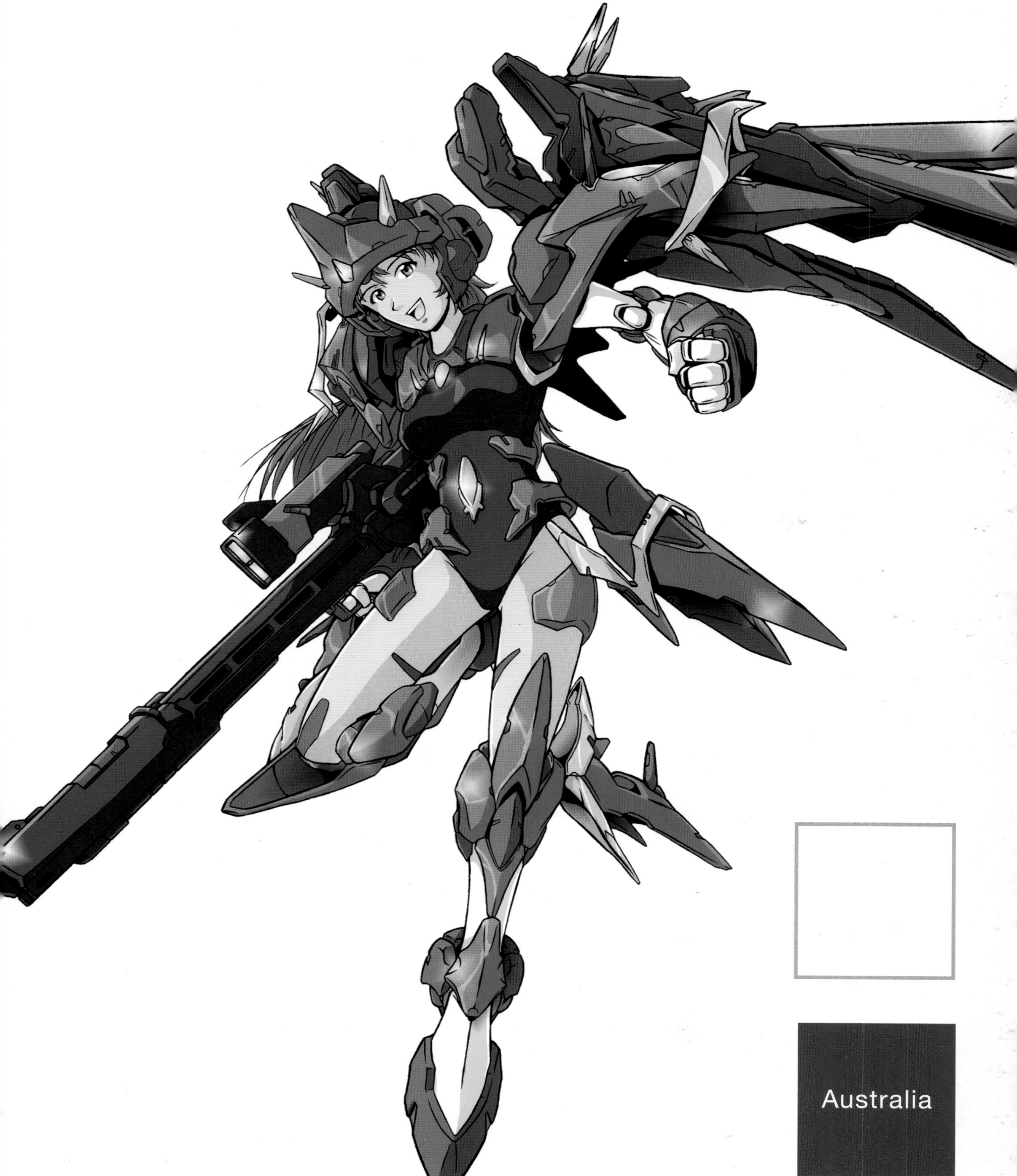

Australia

Chile

You Garmendia Ayala

NEKO-LICIOUS

This candy-colored cat girl

hails from South America,

though the jingle bells in her hair

and the glimmer in her eyes

are homegrown hallmarks

of made-in-Japan manga.

Chile

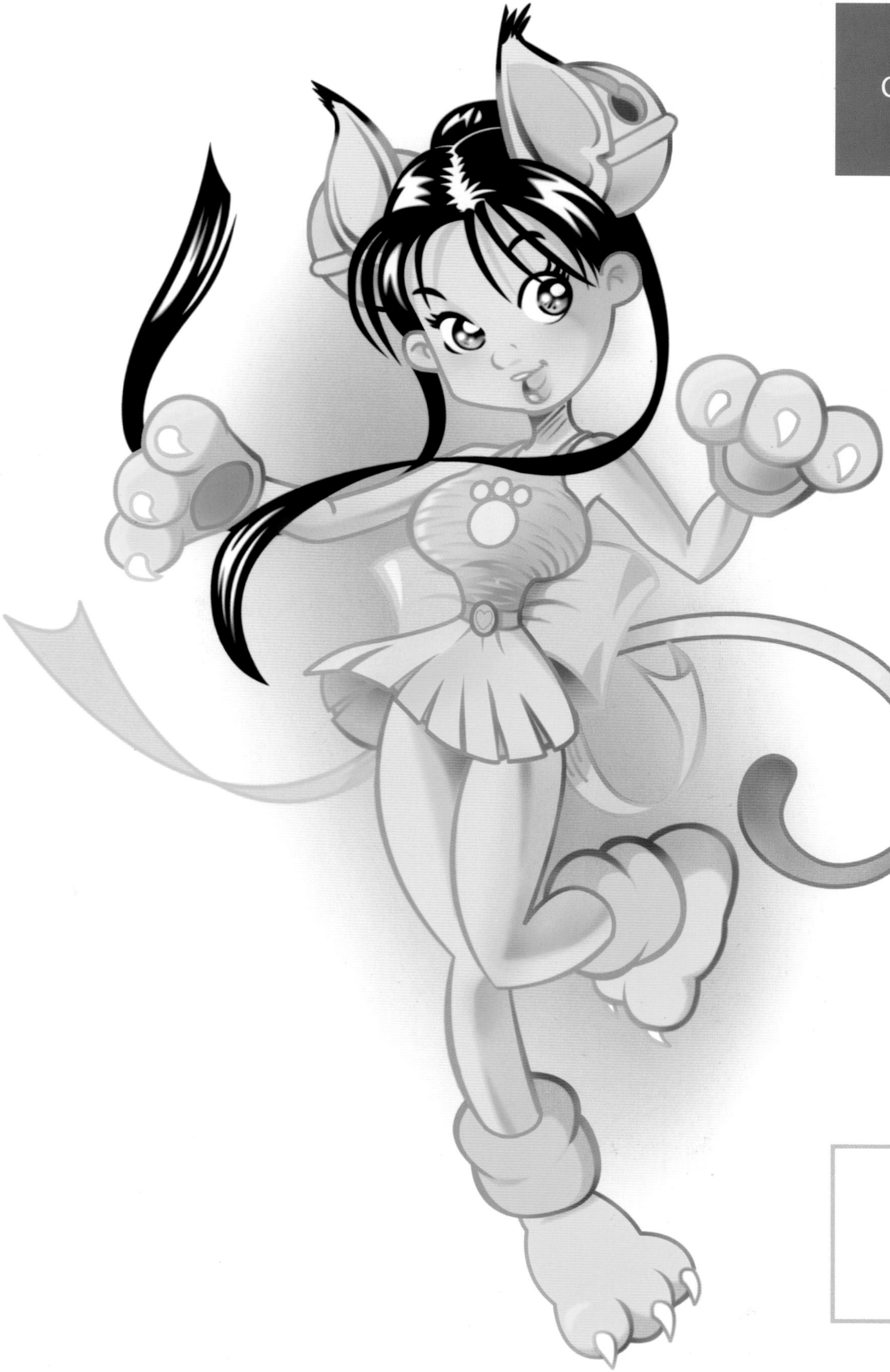

Australia

Michael Li

MOTOR MANGA

Our covergirl is a little bit of everything:
She would blend right into the world
of early Akira Toriyama, but manages
to establish a style all her own.
Skin tones hint at her aboriginal origins,
but the iPod and bike show
she's a city girl at heart.

Australia

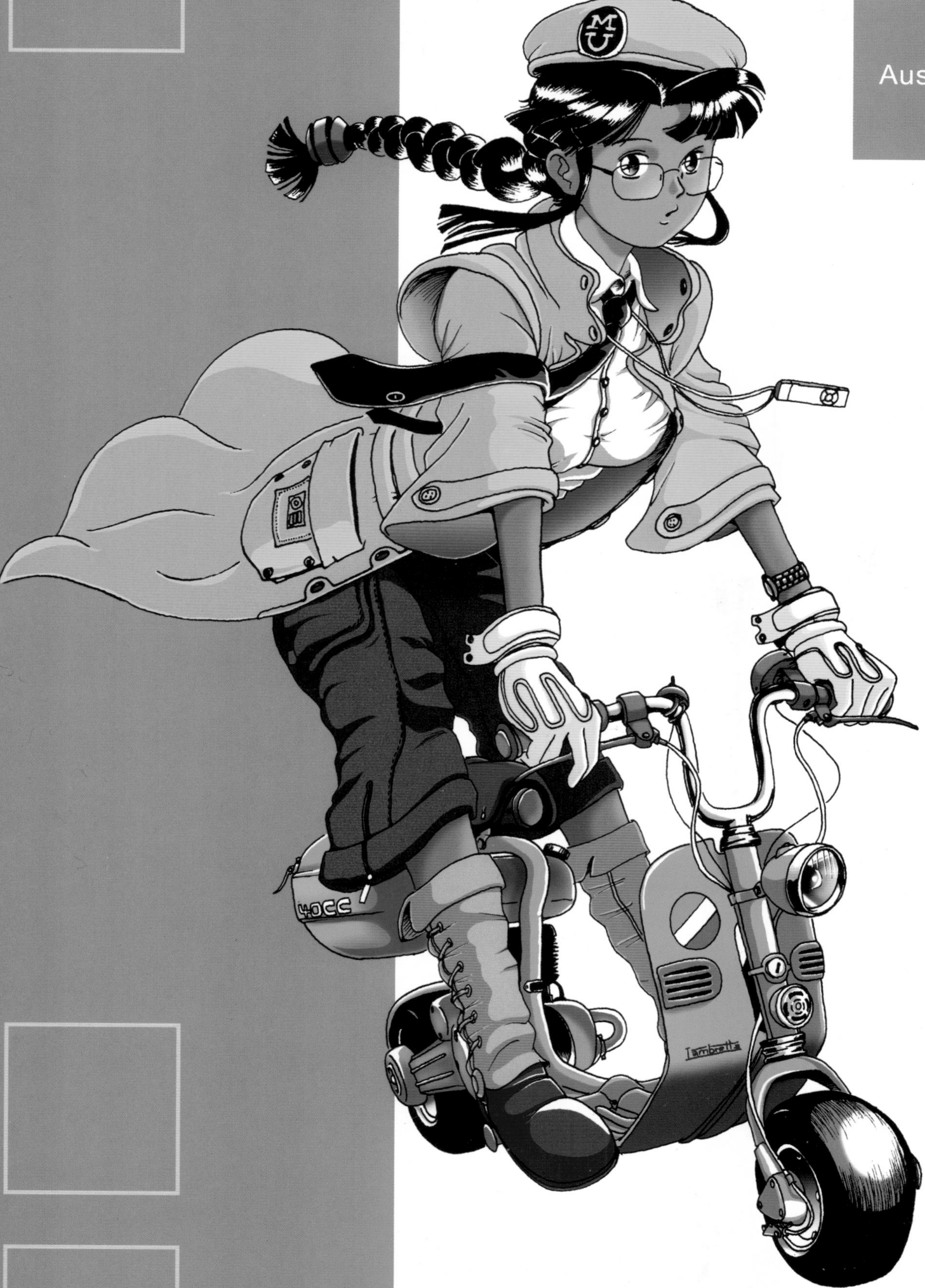
40CC
Lambretta